A
PRACTICAL
GUIDE TO
FINDING
AND USING
YOUR
SPIRITUAL
GIFTS

TYNDALE HOUSE
PUBLISHERS, INC.
WHEATON, ILLINOIS

TIM BLANCHARD

A
PRACTICAL
GUIDE TO

Finding *and using*

Your
Spiritual
Gifts

All Scripture references are from
the *King James Version* of the Bible (KJV)
and from the *New American Standard Bible* (NASB)
unless otherwise noted.

Fifth printing, revised edition, April 1988

Library of Congress Catalog Card Number 82-73453
ISBN 0-8423-4898-0

To my wife, Barbara,
who has consistently
demonstrated to me
the greatest spiritual gift,
love.

CONTENTS

PREFACE 9
INTRODUCTION 11
ONE: Distinguishing Some Terms 15
TWO: Understanding the Gifts 20
THREE: The Trinity at Work in the Gifted Church 32
FOUR: The Trinity at Work with the Gifts 35
FIVE: Studying the Key Passages 37
SIX: Evaluation One: Your Spiritual Interests 43
SEVEN: Evaluation Two: Computerized Spiritual Gifts Inventory (SGI) 54
EIGHT: Evaluation Three: Spiritual Interests Others See in You 73
NINE: Evaluation Four: Past Christian Service Experiences 98
TEN: Evaluating Yourself against Each Gift 100
ELEVEN: Making a Commitment 107
TWELVE: Mobilizing Your Church through Spiritual Gifts 123

APPENDIXES
I Planning a Spiritual Gifts Seminar 130
II Structuring a Spiritual Gifts Seminar 134
III Illustrated Score Sheet for Evaluations One and Three 139
IV Guide to Interpreting the Results of Evaluation One 140
V Guide to Interpreting the Results of Evaluation Three 157

PREFACE

I received my seminary training and began my pastoral ministry during the late 1960s and early 1970s at the height of the evangelical interest in spiritual gifts.

Upon entering my first pastorate, I searched for practical helps to guide our people in determining their spiritual gifts. I did not find in any one book or resource the material I believed was needed. As a result, God led and the Holy Spirit enabled me to forge out this manual.

I acknowledge particularly the helpful background materials developed by my good friends in the ministry: Stu Weber, John Peterson, and Galen Currah. Tapes and seminar materials of Dr. Earl Radmacher, Dr. Gordon McMinn, Dr. Ray Stedman, and Mr. Bill Gothard were also very helpful.

Loren Fischer of Western Conservative Baptist Seminary and Harold Westing of Conservative Baptist Seminary gave essential suggestions and critiques. Without their work, the manual would never have reached this stage of development and completion.

On a very practical level, I owe a great deal to my mother, Mrs. Lillian Blanchard, who spent many hours editing and typing. Finally, I was continually encouraged by the people of West Side Baptist Church, and their interest in finding and using their spiritual gifts. They, especially, have made this project worth the effort.

INTRODUCTION

The place of spiritual gifts in the local church has come a long way in the last fifteen years. At first, attention was given largely to discussions and debates about what the gifts are and which ones are for the twentieth century. Enjoying and using the gifts was definitely of secondary importance. In recent years, however, a better balance between the knowledge about and the use of gifts has been achieved.

The Scripture teaches that every Christian should fit into a spiritual body (the local church), just as physical members unite together in a physical body. This spiritual body needs the equivalent of hands, feet, eyes, joints, and all the other bodily "members." Our spiritual gifts give us insight into what "member" we were designed to be in relation to the Body of Christ. Our challenge is to discover our gifts and become a contributor for the benefit of the whole Body.

At the moment of our spiritual birth, we receive our spiritual gift. However, we have no innate comprehension of what that gift is or even of our having been given it. We must be taught. We are like the boy who, immediately after birth, became heir to a fortune. The fortune became meaningful to him only when he realized that he was an heir with vast resources at his disposal.

Some people today say that the Bible does not emphasize the discovery and development of spiritual gifts, and so, we shouldn't bother to focus on these areas either. This view fails to be convincing when we consider the exhortations in the New Testament regarding spiritual gifts. Without giving attention to gifts, how can we have sound judgment about our place in the church (Romans 12:3), avoid being ignorant about gifts (1 Corinthians 12:1), be good stewards of our gifts (1 Peter 4:10), and abound in their use for the strengthening of the church (1 Corinthians 14:12)?

In addition, since the gifted leaders in the church are to equip the saints to serve and the basis for such service is the possession of their gifts, it is logically impossible to reach the goal without the leaders being aware of the members' gifts (Ephesians 4:11–13). Finally, Paul exhorted

Timothy not to neglect his gift (1 Timothy 4:14) and not to grow stale in its use (2 Timothy 1:6). If Timothy wasn't supposed to be thinking about giftedness but only about "serving the Lord," then he couldn't have responded to Paul's exhortations. Everything considered, Christians—members and leaders of the church—have to be thinking about gifts in order to respond properly to the scriptural guidance about effective service in their local churches.

Every thinking, full-time church worker knows that many ministries lie untouched because of the inactivity of some Christians. He also sees that the uninvolved do not move to maturity as quickly as those who are happily serving. How can these gifted but idle people be rallied to serve? Each must know his or her gift, and each must be properly motivated to rise up and meet a need.

For years, pastors and Christian leaders have encouraged workers to "get involved"—with only a fair degree of success. "Won't you give prayerful consideration to these needs that we have placed before you today?" Such pleas have abounded. Emphasis has been placed on recruiting techniques, spiritual arm-twisting, and emotional appeals. With these methods, one wonders how many parts of the spiritual body have been doing tasks designed for *other* parts to do.

Psychologist Leo MacManus declares that motivation comes alive when a person: a) gains recognition by others, b) enjoys a sense of accomplishment, c) is impressed with the importance of the task he is doing, and d) holds a definite responsibility. Uninvolved people experience none of these motivators. They must take hold of the most exciting catalyst for involvement—spiritual gifts.

Every inactive member must be informed that he has a special, spiritual, God-given gift. When he sees that his gift is essential for the proper functioning of the church, the member immediately begins to feel biblically based recognition. Upon discovering his gift, his spiritual self-worth increases greatly. Training then builds confidence. Finally, he begins shouldering responsibilities and becomes increasingly inspired by a sense of personal accomplishment through doing an important task. A believer who properly understands and uses his spiritual gift becomes an enthusiastic worker.

This manual is a learning tool. It is intended to direct you, a gifted believer, on a course toward finding, understanding, and using your spiritual gift. The impact can be revolutionary. Why? Because spiritual gifts are God's way of equipping his believers to minister in his church. All other methods are inferior.

Paul charged the Corinthians, "Now, concerning spiritual gifts, brethren, I would not have you ignorant" (1 Corinthians 12:1, KJV). We must be faithful leaders and workers who heed this mandate.

(For those who would like to use these studies for a spiritual gifts seminar or as a Sunday school class quarter study, see Appendixes I and II, which discuss how to plan and structure such group studies.)

ONE
Distinguishing
Some Terms

NATURAL TALENTS. Natural talents are inherited abilities and interests received at birth. "He's a natural athlete," says a proud mother, "just like his dad." Such talents become more obvious through education, training, and practice. Spiritual life is not necessary for their development.

These inborn abilities are often used in church work by dedicated Christians. However, they must be clearly distinguished from spiritual gifts. A Christian's spiritual gift may appear similar to one of his talents. However, the inner motivation will be different. And the degree and quality of effectiveness will also be different.

From the following biblical examples, write down the name of the person and his natural talent.

	Name	Natural talent
Genesis 4:2	Eve	child bearing
Genesis 4:20	Jabel	leader of shepherds
Genesis 4:21	Jubal	leader of musicians
Genesis 4:22	Tubal-Cain	maker of tools
Genesis 25:27	Esau	skillful hunter

NORMAL SPIRIT-CONTROLLED BEHAVIOR. When a person accepts the Lord Jesus Christ as his personal Savior, ". . . he is a new creature: old things are passed away; behold, all things are become new" (2 Corinthians 5:17, KJV). This new life is possible because the Holy Spirit of God indwells him (1 Corinthians 6:19). He has the responsibility to learn and obey the Scriptures, confess all known sin, and let the Spirit of God control his life. In so doing, his heart and soul, including natural talents, become a channel through which the Spirit can work.

The resulting Spirit-controlled attitudes and actions of the believer, such as love, joy, temperance, witnessing, giving, and exercising faith, are spiritual fruit. All Christians can and should bear these fruits—reveal these qualities—regardless of temperament, abilities, or spiritual gifts.

From the following verses, note the ways the Spirit-controlled life will be demonstrated.

1 Thessalonians 5:11 _Encourage + build each other up_
Galatians 5:13 _serve one another in love_
Hebrews 10:25 _meet + encourage one another_
2 Corinthians 9:7 _be a cheerful giver_
2 Corinthians 5:7 _live by faith_
1 John 4:1 _test the spirits to see if they are from God_

Is it enough to be a Spirit-filled Christian who uses his natural talents for the Lord? No! There is more to the Christian life.

SPIRITUAL GIFTS. A spiritual gift is a supernatural gift of grace which is measured and given out by God to each true Christian as a stewardship for serving the church of Jesus Christ. Just as we receive our natural talents at the time of our first birth, so we receive our spiritual gift at the time of our second birth into spiritual life (1 Peter 4:10). Each gift is in the form of a specific spiritual ability for service. With it, the believer is to help build up the church and honor God. To be all that God desires, a Christian must know and use his spiritual gift.

This gift may, in certain cases, seem similar to our natural talents. It may also appear to be just the natural outcome of Spirit-controlled behavior. However, the Scriptures clearly label a spiritual gift as a distinct, special present from the Holy Spirit. We must realize that effective service in the church depends upon the proper understanding and use of our spiritual gift.

In the New Testament, two Greek words are translated "spiritual gifts." One is _neumatika_ (1 Corinthians 12:1), from _neuma,_ meaning "breath or spirit." This term emphasizes the inner spiritual motivation that comes with the gift.

The other word is _charismata_ (Romans 12:6), from _charis,_ meaning grace. This term emphasizes God's grace (unmerited love of God to man) in outward display. By grace, the gifted believer is capable of demonstrating spiritual ability in the church, where all can see. It is God who provides both the inner motivation for, and the outward expression of, a person's spiritual gift.

Prior to Pentecost, the Spirit of God indwelt God-fearing

believers only in certain instances. He was more normally "upon" them (Numbers 11:17), and "among" them (Haggai 2:5). However, the Spirit did enter mightily into some select Old Testament servants, indwelling, filling, and gifting them for service by a single divine act. Indicate below the names of six such persons and the type of spiritual gift each received.

	Name	Gift
Genesis 41:38	Joseph – spirit of God – charge of Egypt
Exodus 31:3, 6	Bezaleb + Oholiab – artistic craftsmen
Numbers 11:25, 26	Eldad + Medad – prophesied
Numbers 27:18-20	Joshua – lead Israelites
Deuteronomy 34:9	Joshua – wisdom
Daniel 4:8b, 18	Belteshazzar – interpreter

These occasions of indwelling and gifting seem to be forerunners of the Church Age. Today, in the Church Age, all believers are indwelt by the Spirit, and all are gifted for service.

Three main lists of spiritual gifts are recorded in the New Testament. From the Scripture verses below, list the gifts you see in these key passages:

Romans 12:6-8
1. prophesying – use in proportion to your faith
2. serving
3. Teaching
4. encouraging
5. contributing to the needs of others
6. leadership
7. showing mercy

1 Corinthians 12:8-10
1. message of wisdom from the spirit
2. knowledge
3. faith
4. gift of healing
5. miraculous powers
6. prophecy
7. distinguishing between spirits
8. speaking in different kind of tongues
9. interpretation of tongues

1 Corinthians 12:28-30
1. Apostles – appointed

17

2. _prophets_
3. _teachers_
4. _workers of miracles_
5. _Those having gifts of healing_
6. _" able to help others_
7. _" with gifts of administration_
8. _" speaking in different tongues_

Two main categories of gifts are included in these passages. One group is made up of those which emphasize outward demonstrations which are clearly miraculous in nature. God gave them to the early church without preparation or development by the recipient. There are four such gifts listed above. List them below:

1. _wisdom, knowledge - teachers_
2. _prophecy_
3. _mercy - healing sick_
4. _tongues_

Gifts in the second category are supernatural because God gives the ability, energy, and productivity for them. However, they do not show themselves so clearly to be miraculous in nature. Thirteen such gifts are listed above, some of them in more than one passage. List the thirteen below:

1. _faith_
2. _tongues_
3. _able to help others_
4. _gifts of administration_
5. _serving_
6. _teaching_
7. _encouraging_
8. _leadership_
9. _____
10. _____
11. _____
12. _____
13. _____

In addition to the above lists, several gifts are listed in Ephesians 4:11. They are sometimes called "office" gifts because they are thought of as positions in the church. They may be filled by persons showing any one of a number of spiritual gifts. For example, an evangelist may

18

have the gift of preaching, exhortation, or possibly another speaking gift through which evangelism is accomplished. List the five "office" gifts below:

1. _apostles_
2. _prophets_
3. _evangelists_
4. _pastors_
5. _teachers_

Much of the writing about spiritual gifts has centered on the continuing debate regarding the four miraculous gifts and the five "office" gifts. The complex exegetical and theological issues involved in this debate can only be resolved by detailed studies. It is not the intent of this study to enter into these highly controversial areas. Our purpose is to assist the concerned Christian in determining which of the thirteen spiritual gifts he has. These gifts lend themselves to testing, evaluation, and service.

TWO
Understanding the Gifts

The first step toward discovering one's spiritual gift is to know what the gifts are. This may be accomplished in two ways. First, the biblical meaning of the words used to describe the gifts must be understood. This requires an analysis of the New Testament Greek words from which they are translated.

Second, the practical New Testament meaning of the words must be grasped. This is done by examining several passages in which the words are used. Insights from these passages will show what can be expected from the exercise of each gift.

Following is an examination of word meanings, together with illustrations from Scripture. Study the words, then answer the questions under "New Testament Insights."

GIFT OF PROPHECY (PREACHING)
Word meaning

The biblical word "prophecy" (Romans 12:6) is translated from the Greek compound word, *prophateia*, which is made up of two parts: *pro*, "forth, for"; and *phateia*, "to speak." These parts combine to mean "to speak forth," or, in the noun form, "something spoken forth or one speaking forth." In the Old Testament, the prophets were God's mouthpiece for speaking forth his truth and his will to the people.

In the New Testament, there were prophets who spoke revelation to the infant church for the purpose of providing a foundation for the church (Ephesians 2:19-21). Later, others with the gift of prophecy spoke forth the Scripture with great conviction. The person with this gift strongly proclaimed the Scriptures with a view to seeing lives changed (1 Corinthians 14:3).

The gift of prophecy is evident in certain preachers today. The basic feature of speaking forth God's truth with strong feeling is still primary. However, since prophesying is a gift and not a position, professional preachers are not the only ones with the gift.

20

New Testament insights

1. What did the New Testament prophets do that indicated their gift?
   a. Luke 7:39 *should know who's touching him - feel sinners - pierces sinners*
   b. Acts 11:28 *predict future*
   c. 1 Corinthians 14:24, 25 *everybody prophesying except sinners*
2. What specific inner motivations and goals did those with the gift of prophecy have?
   a. Acts 15:32 *encourage + strengthen brothers*
   b. 1 Corinthians 14:3 *strengthening encouragement + comfort*
3. From Acts 13:1-5, what was Barnabas' and Saul's position and task (verse 1)? *do the work of the Holy Spirit*
   a. What did they do when they ministered (verse 5)? *proclaimed the word of God to the Jewish people*
   b. Prophecy means "to speak forth" and preaching means "to herald the message." What do the two terms have in common? *Both are telling the good news of God*
4. As the New Testament was being completed, what provided the foundation for the prophet's proclamation? (See 2 Peter 1:19-21.) *words from the Holy Spirit*
5. How are true and false prophets distinguished?
   a. Deuteronomy 18:20-22 *if what a prophet says doesn't happen or come true*
   b. Matthew 7:15, 16 *you will recognize by good deeds + words*
   c. Matthew 24:23, 24 *false prophets will try to deceive you by signs + miracles*

GIFT OF TEACHING

Word meaning

   The biblical word "teaching" (Romans 12:7) is translated from the Greek word *didasko,* meaning "to teach." The word has a very broad spectrum of meanings. It involves learning and understanding an area of knowledge. Also, it involves helping others to get from where they are in their understanding to where the teacher is.

   The gifted teacher is one with great energy. He is concerned with designing and using the most effective methods for helping others to grasp truth. He is concerned with making the truth valuable for daily living.

New Testament insights

1. What was the central emphasis in all early church teaching? (See Acts 15:35; 18:11.) *teaching word of God*
2. What is the person with the gift of teaching concerned about? *teaching to as many people as possible*

21

a. Acts 18:26 _listeners went to inform teacher more accurately_
b. Colossians 1:28; 3:16, 17_____

3. How would you distinguish preaching from teaching? Both are mentioned together in various passages.
   a. Acts 5:42 _taught everywhere people would listen_
   b. Acts 15:35 _stayed in one city_
4. What concern bears on the heart of the truly gifted teacher? (See James 3:1.) _being judged more strictly_

GIFT OF WORD OF KNOWLEDGE
Word meaning

The biblical word "knowledge" (1 Corinthians 12:8) is translated from the Greek word *ginosis.* It is the noun form of the often-used verb *ginosko,* "to know by observation [sight] and experience." It is to be distinguished from the other word for knowing, *oida,* "to know by the gathering and use of information" (having "heard").

One having the spiritual gift of the word of knowledge has a motivation for knowing the content of Scripture in detail. He understands and arranges truth carefully. The Holy Spirit enables him to have the proper balance and emphasis in viewing Scripture as a whole.

New Testament insights

From the following verses, indicate the areas of study which the one with the gift of the word of knowledge will develop:
1. Luke 1:76-79 _spread word of salvation_
2. Philippians 3:8 _give up all things for Christ_
3. 1 Corinthians 2:9-13 _Spiritual truths_
4. 2 Corinthians 10:5_____

GIFT OF WORD OF WISDOM
Word meaning

The biblical word "wisdom" (1 Corinthians 12:8) is translated from the Greek word *sophia,* meaning "wisdom," which derives from a root word meaning "to taste." This ties wisdom to experiential living rather than just to theory. Wisdom is the special ability to take a number of truths and use them to judge "gray areas" not directly resolved by a single truth.

One with the spiritual gift of wisdom and training demonstrates an unusual ability in the church to make discerning applications to practical questions on Christian living.

New Testament insights
1. The gift of wisdom will be based on what foundation?
   a. 1 Corinthians 1:23, 24, 30 *God*

   b. Ephesians 1:17 *Spirit of wisdom*
2. Characterize godly wisdom as shown in James 3:17. Then expand the meaning of each term to show how it helps a person be wise.
   a. *wisdom from heaven is pure*
   b. *peace loving*
   c. *considerate*
   d. *submissive*
   e. *full of mercy*
   f. *good fruit*
   g. *impartial*
   h. *sincere*
3. Using the Scripture verses below, indicate what words of wisdom can do for a church.
   a. Romans 16:19 *obedience, wise about what is good + innocent of evil*
   b. Ephesians 5:15, 17 *be wise - know God's will*
   c. 2 Timothy 3:15 *faith in Jesus Christ*

GIFT OF EXHORTATION
Word meaning

The biblical word "exhortation" (Romans 12:8) is translated from the compound Greek word *paraklasis,* which is made up of the following two parts: *para,* "beside, alongside"; and *klasis,* "to call." The parts combine to mean "to call alongside"; or, in the noun form, "one called alongside another." In the broadest sense, one can be called alongside another for any number of reasons. The Bible narrows down the reasons for coming alongside to: (a) helping in a project, (b) embracing proper faith action, and (c) comforting others.

One with the spiritual gift of exhortation has the inner motivation and desire to encourage and comfort others in the above ways.

New Testament insights

1. What is the main resource for their exhortations? (See Romans 15:4.) *written scripture*
2. What is the burden of the exhorter's heart?
   a. Acts 2:40 *save yourself from corruption*
   b. Acts 11:23 *remain true to God*
3. What are some of the areas of life the New Testament exhorters spoke of in the exercise of exhortation?
   a. 1 Thessalonians 2:11, 12 *encourage - comforter*
   b. 1 Thessalonians 5:14 *encourage timid, help weak, warn idle, be patient with everyone*
   c. Titus 1:9 *hold firmly to trustworthy msg & encourage others*
   d. Hebrews 3:13 *encourage daily*
4. Barnabas was a classic example of a comforting, building exhorter. Note his special ministry to one man and the result. (See Acts 15:37-40; 2 Timothy 4:11.)_____

GIFT OF FAITH

Word meaning

The biblical word "faith" (1 Corinthians 12:9) is translated from one of the most common and basic New Testament words, *pistis,* which means "a trust or conviction about something or someone." As a spiritual gift, faith is confidence in God's wonder-working power. In 1 Corinthians 13:2 Paul writes: ". . . and though I have all faith *[pistis]* so that I could remove mountains . . ."

One with the spiritual gift of faith has vision and foresight. He demonstrates unusual confidence and boldness (Hebrews 11:1). Those with this gift serve to propel the body of believers into actively claiming the promises of God. Even when the church faces seemingly insurmountable problems, he is optimistic.

New Testament insights

1. Note some of the things accomplished by Old Testament saints who exercised great faith. (See Hebrews 11:33, 34.)_____

2. Read Acts 6:5-8. List the ways the gospel flourished through these men who were "full of faith."_____

24

3. Read Acts 11:22-24. Barnabas' faith produced what result in Christians and non-Christians?_____

_____

GIFT OF DISCERNMENT OF SPIRITS
Word meaning

The biblical phrase "discerning of spirits" (1 Corinthians 12:10) is translated from the Greek words *diakrisis . . . pneumaton. Diakrisis* is a compound word made up of two parts: *dia,* "through"; and *krisis,* "to judge, divide, distinguish." The parts combine to mean one who "judges or distinguishes through a situation to a decision." *Pneumaton* is the normal word for spirits. When combined with *diakrisis,* it speaks of the process of judging through a person's speech and actions to discern the spirit behind them.

A person with the spiritual gift of discernment of spirits demonstrates a unique ability to correctly judge the true spiritual level and integrity of others.

New Testament insights
1. What two criteria are important for developing the gift of discernment of spirits? (See Hebrews 5:13, 14.)_____

_____

_____

2. What will be the inner drive of the one with this gift? (See 1 Thessalonians 5:21.)_____

_____

3. From the following passages, write down the situation briefly and the evidence of discernment of spirits.
   a. Acts 5:1-5_____

   _____

   b. Acts 8:18–23_____

   _____

   c. Acts 13:8-11_____

   _____

   d. Acts 16:16-18_____

   _____

   _____

4. Why is the gift of discernment of spirits so necessary in our day?
   a. 1 John 4:1-3_____
   b. 1 Timothy 4:1_____

   _____

GIFT OF HELPS
Word meaning

   The biblical word "helps" (1 Corinthians 12:28) is translated from the compound Greek word *antilapsis*. The word is made up of two parts: *anti,* "opposite, instead of and in exchange for"; and *lambano,* "to grasp, seize, or take up helpfully." The parts combine to mean in the noun form, "to seize something in front of one for the purpose of helping." This implies responding to a request to do a certain job. Such usage was prevalent in early papyrus writings.

   One with the spiritual gift of helps responds when a need becomes clearly known and a request for help is given.

New Testament insights

   From the Scriptures below, describe some of the people with this gift and what they did.
   1. Acts 20:35 *more blessed to give than receive*
   2. 1 Timothy 6:2_____
   3. 2 Timothy 1:16_____
   4. 1 Corinthians 16:15_____

   _____

GIFT OF SERVING (MINISTRY)
Word meaning

   The biblical word for "serving" or "ministry" (Romans 12:7) is translated from the Greek word *diakonos.* The word "deacon" in the New Testament comes directly from it. It is probably derived from the verb *dioko,* "to hasten after, pursue."

   There are many Greek words translated "service." One emphasizes the subjection of the server to his master; another, the willingness to serve due to high respect; and another, service for wages. In contrast, *diakonos* conveys the idea of very special and personal service rendered to another in love.

   One with the spiritual gift of serving is motivated to

initiate service for another in the body of Christ. He will serve diligently in love.

New Testament insights

From the Scripture verses below, describe some of the qualities, activities, and results of one having the gift of serving:
1. Luke 10:40_____
2. Luke 22:27_____
3. Acts 6:1-3_____
4. Romans 16:1, 2_____
5. 1 Corinthians 16:15-18_____
6. Colossians 4:7, 8_____

_____

GIFT OF ADMINISTRATION (GOVERNMENTS)

Word meaning

The biblical word "governments" (1 Corinthians 12:28) is translated from the Greek word *kubernesis,* meaning "to guide, govern." It was specifically used of a helmsman of a ship. His position was the most important in determining the direction of the ship (James 3:4).

One with the spiritual gift of administration or government manifests the wisdom, tact, and decisiveness to give guidance to one or many aspects of the church work.

New Testament insights

The only New Testament uses of the word other than that in 1 Corinthians 12:28 are Acts 27:11 and Revelation 18:17, both of which refer to the "master" of a ship. Using the account in Acts 27:11-20; 27-29; 38-44, write down the decisions made by the master helmsman during the storm.

1. _____
2. _____
3. _____
4. _____
5. _____
6. _____
7. _____
8. _____
9. _____
10. _____
11. _____

12. _____
13. _____
14. _____

Obviously the helmsman in the above situation was operating under great stress. Had he obeyed Paul's early warning not to start out on the journey, he would not have had the problems. However, from the list of decisions the helmsman made, draw out some principles that a gifted administrator in a church should use. Some of the principles may be derived from what the helmsman did wrong.

1. _____
2. _____
3. _____
4. _____
5. _____
6. _____
7. _____
8. _____

GIFT OF RULING
Word meaning

The biblical word "ruling" (Romans 12:8) is translated from the compound Greek word *prohistame,* made up of the following two parts: *pro,* "before"; and *histame,* "to stand." The parts combine to mean "to stand before" others for the purpose of overseeing or directing work.

One with the spiritual gift of ruling manifests the confidence, desire, and skills required to lead a group.

New Testament insights
1. How should the ruler rule? (See 1 Timothy 3:4, 5, 12.)___
   manage his own family well if he can't do that how can he take care of God's church)
2. What characterizes the ruler's leadership? (See 1 Thessalonians 5:12, 13.)_____
3. What is one of the ongoing tasks of the ruler? (See Titus 1:5.) *____ faith* _____
4. What is the foundation for proper ruling? (See 1 Timothy 5:17.)_____

GIFT OF MERCY
Word meaning

The biblical word "mercy" (Romans 12:8) is translated

28

from the Greek word *eleon,* meaning "mercy, pathos."
Webster's dictionary defines pathos as "the quality in
something experienced or observed which arouses feelings
of pity, sorrow, sympathy, or compassion." These feelings
provide the motivation for action in one with this gift.

One with the spiritual gift of mercy cheerfully
demonstrates in action compassion for those that are sick
or in misery, either physically or spiritually.

New Testament insights

1. What actions constituted acts of mercy in the following
   passages?
   a. From Luke 10:30-37, indicate the progression of four
      specific actions taken by this merciful man.
      1) _____
      2) _____
      3) _____
      4) _____
   b. Philippians 2:1-3_____
2. What attitude should characterize acts of mercy? (See
   Romans 12:8.) *to do it cheerfully*
3. What should be the outstanding motivation for acting in
   mercy toward others? (See Titus 3:5.)_____

_____

GIFT OF GIVING

Word meaning

The biblical word "giving" (Romans 12:8) is translated
from the compound Greek word *metadidomi.* It is made up
of two parts: *meta,* "in the midst of, in association or
fellowship"; and *didomi,* "to give." The parts combine to
mean "to give in association with others." It implies that
the giving is not done objectively or coldly, but within the
context of a spiritual relationship.

There is fellowship with God in giving as an act of
worship. There is fellowship with others when giving is
done in love and concern for the needy.

One with the spiritual gift of giving has the inner
motivation and desire to share in others' needs by giving
of himself, his material goods and money.

New Testament insights

1. What is the main viewpoint to have in exercising the
   gift of giving? (See 2 Corinthians 8:4.)_____

_____

2. What is the main purpose for the gift of giving in the body of Christ? (See Ephesians 4:28.)_____
_____

3. What kind of needs are met by one with the gift of giving?
   a. Matthew 6:1-4_____
   b. Luke 3:11_____
   c. Acts 11:27-30_____
4. What are some of the attitudes toward giving that we might expect to see in someone with the gift?
   a. 2 Corinthians 8:12_____
   b. 2 Corinthians 9:7_____
   c. 2 Corinthians 9:13_____

HOW MANY GIFTS DO I HAVE? A central question which has not yet been totally resolved by biblical scholars is: Is it possible for a believer to have more than one unique spiritual gift? A brief survey of the Scriptures involved will suffice to show that every believer has at least one spiritual gift.

In 1 Peter 4:10 (NASB), Peter writes, ". . . as each one has received a special gift . . ." In addition, the body metaphor, as developed by Paul in 1 Corinthians 12:12-27, Romans 12:4, 5 and Ephesians 4:12-16, emphasizes that the gifted members of the church are similar to the functioning parts of the physical body. Each physical member of the body has a unique function to fulfill for the proper working of the body. Likewise, it is argued, each spiritual member of the spiritual body, the church, has a unique function (as a spiritually gifted believer) to fulfill for the proper working of the whole spiritual body.

In addition, those who believe that every Christian has just one gift point out that the word "severally" in 1 Corinthians 12:11 (". . . the selfsame Spirit, dividing to every man severally as he will," KJV), should be translated "individually." This removes the implication from the verse that the Spirit may give several gifts to one believer.

Others believe that a Christian may have more than one spiritual gift. They appeal to the fact that Paul, for example, had a number of spiritual gifts, such as prophecy, teaching, miracles, tongues, etc. They argue that in using the body metaphor, Paul was simply trying to show the interrelationship and necessity of the various spiritual gifts in the church. They contend he was not trying to speak to the issue of the number of gifts one member in that body might have.

Finally, those who believe that a Christian may have more than one gift take 1 Corinthians 12:31 ("But covet earnestly the best gifts," KJV) as an imperative command to seek the best gifts. If it is possible to seek gifts (plural) and receive them, it must also be possible to have more than one gift by such seeking.

The above discussion will suffice to show the nature of the debate on the issue. For purposes of this study, reference will be made to "gift" rather than to "gifts" since we are confident that each believer has at least one spiritual gift.

THREE
The Trinity at Work
in the Gifted Church

All three Persons of the eternal Godhead—God the Father,
God the Son, and God the Holy Spirit—are involved in
spiritual gifts. This is a clear testimony to their unity in
essence and purpose and yet their distinctiveness in
personality and activity. While they have the same eternal
attributes, each of the three Persons has unique ministries
which distinguish him from the others. An understanding
of the Trinity's working is an essential foundation for
putting spiritual gifts in proper perspective.

In this chapter we shall study the members of the
Trinity as they are revealed in the major passages on
spiritual gifts. Other passages will be included only for
expansion and clarification.

GOD THE FATHER

1. In Ephesians 4:6, the word "all" refers to the believers
   in the "one body" mentioned in 4:4. Therefore, God is
   the Father of all the individuals in the church body.
   From verse 6, list the four ways God is related to all
   the believers. Then, using the additional verses given,
   explain some of the details of his leadership.

   a. _Father of all, who is over all → through all + in all_
      Ephesians 1:2, 3. _blessed all_
      Ephesians 2:19 _members of God's household_

      Ephesians 3:14, 15_____

      2 Corinthians 6:17, 18_____

   b. _above all_
      Psalm 57:5_____
      James 1:17_____

   c. _Through all_
      1 Corinthians 8:6_____

      1 Timothy 2:5_____

   d. _in all_

John 14:17_____

1 Corinthians 6:19_____

2. What attribute of God the Father makes him willing to exercise headship over men by a personal relationship with them? (See Romans 12:1a.) *offer your bodies as a living spiritual act of worship*

   a. Did God have to provide for this relationship?
   2 Peter 2:4-7_____

   Titus 3:3-7_____

   b. What is the key character quality the Father desires to develop in those with whom he has a relationship? (See Leviticus 11:44.) *Consecrate yourselves & be holy*

3. The way in which God's mercy is displayed in the church is worked out in what is called his *rebirth*_____ (Romans 12:2).

GOD THE SON

1. To fulfill God's will within the church, the believer must first commit himself to what position concerning Jesus Christ? (See 1 Corinthians 12:3.) *believer filled with the Holy Spirit*

   a. What is involved in making and keeping this commitment?
   Luke 6:46 *Do what the Lord says*
   John 11:27 *believe*
   2 Corinthians 6:17 *Come out & be separate*
   Colossians 1:10 *grow in the knowledge*

2. What two main goals should every Christian strive for in his relationship with Christ? (See Ephesians 4:13).

   a. *reach unity in faith & knowledge of the Son of God*
   Ephesians 4:3-6_____

   Ephesians 1:17_____

   Philippians 3:8-10_____

   b. _____
   John 1:14_____

3. What are the respective tasks of Christ and Christians within the church?

a. Ephesians 4:15, 16_____

_____

b. Acts 2:47_____

_____

c. Romans 12:5_____

_____

d. 1 Corinthians 12:27_____

_____

GOD THE HOLY SPIRIT
1. What is the Spirit's contribution toward the believer's
entrance into the body of Christ?
   a. John 3:5 *no one will enter the kingdom*
   unless he is born of water + the Spirit
   b. 1 Corinthians 12:13_____

_____

2. What is the Holy Spirit's main goal in working with
gifted believers in the body of Christ? (See Ephesians
4:3.) *make every effort to keep the unity*
of the Spirit through the bond
of peace

SUMMARY
   Summarize briefly the main tasks of the Father, Son,
and Holy Spirit pertaining to the Christian in the church.

God the Father:

_____

_____

_____

_____

God the Son:

_____

_____

_____

_____

God the Holy Spirit:

_____

_____

_____

_____

FOUR
The Trinity at Work
with the Gifts

The Trinity is at work not only in the growth and
development of the Church, but also in the introduction
and integration of the spiritual gifts into local churches.
Study the verses which indicate the Trinity's involvement
in establishing a church of gifted believers. Explain briefly
the meaning of each verse.

GOD THE FATHER
1. Romans 12:3 _Don't put yourself above others, judge_
yourself by the faith given you by God
2. 1 Corinthians 12:6 _some one gifted in_
different ways
3. 1 Corinthians 12:18 _God created you the_
way he wants you to be
4. 1 Corinthians 12:24 _____

GOD THE SON
1. 1 Corinthians 12:5 _There is only one God_

GOD THE HOLY SPIRIT
1. 1 Corinthians 12:4, 11 _he determines who_
gets what gifts

SUMMARY
Summarize in the most logical progression (starting with
first things first) the six contributions of the Trinity
toward establishing the gift of each believer in the church
body.
1. _____
2. _____
3. _____
4. _____
5. _____
6. _____

At what points in this process can the believer thwart
what the Godhead wants to do with his gift in the church?
1. _____

35

2. _____

3. _____

4. _____

What do you think happens to a church when contributions by the Trinity cannot materialize due to a believer's inactivity?_____

_____

_____

FIVE
Studying
the Key Passages

Four key passages in the New Testament give us the main biblical principles about thirteen spiritual gifts and their part in the church. These texts are Romans 12:1-8; 1 Corinthians 12:1-31; Ephesians 4:1-16; and 1 Peter 4:7-11. We shall study these passages under three topical headings. In addition, other individual verses where spiritual gifts (charismata) are referred to will be examined to gain as complete a biblical understanding as possible.

PERSONAL PREPARATION BEFORE USING SPIRITUAL GIFTS

1. What four critical commitments must be made before a person should try to determine his spiritual gift? (See Romans 12:1-3.)
   a. *Offer your body as a living sacrifice - act of worship*
   b. *be transformed by the renewing of your mind*
   c. *do not think of yourself above others*
   d. _____

2. What Jewish practice was in Paul's thinking in Romans 12:1 when he wrote, "present your bodies"? (See Luke 2:22.) *Bring it before the altar of God*

3. How can we parallel today the presentation explained in Luke 2:22, since we no longer do that? *baptizing of babies*

4. A "living sacrifice" (Romans 12:1) is a contradiction in terms unless one can die and still be alive. In what sense is the consecrated believer alive and dead? (See Romans 6:6-9, 11-13.)_____

5. What is "acceptable unto God" (Romans 12:1) in a New Testament life sacrifice? (See Acts 10:35.) *accepts all men who fear him & do what is right*

6. What does it mean to be "conformed" to this world? (Romans 12:2.)
   a. Ephesians 2:2, 3_____

37

b. 1 John 2:16 _____

7. A transformation is what takes place in a caterpillar when it goes through metamorphosis and becomes a butterfly. It is an inner transformation with an outer manifestation. How does the inner, spiritual transformation take place in the consecrated believer in Jesus Christ?
   a. Romans 12:2b _____
   b. Philippians 4:8 _____
   _____
   _____

✓ 8. While the transformation process is going on, we should be able to determine with confidence the will of God. How can we know the will of God? What specific things are the will of God?
   a. John 7:17 _____
   _____
   b. 1 Thessalonians 4:3 _____
   c. 1 Thessalonians 5:18 _____
   d. 1 Peter 2:15 _____

9. What characterizes a "worthy" walk for the believer in relationship to his local church? (See Ephesians 4:2.) To the right of your answer, give the positive results of such a walk in the church life; give also the negative results of doing the opposite.

	Positive	*Negative*
a. Humble		
b. Gentle		
c. Patient		
d. Bearing w/ one another		

10. Peter gives four essential qualities in 1 Peter 4:7-9 as preliminary considerations before discussing the use of one's spiritual gift. List them and explain briefly what each quality means, using a dictionary to define the terms.
   a. Be clear minded + self-controlled so you can pray.
   b. _____

c. _Love each other deeply, love covers a multitude of sins_

d. _Offer hospitality without grumbling_

11. Note briefly how each of the qualities in question 10 will help one in finding and/or using his spiritual gift.

    a. _____

    _____

    b. _____

    _____

    c. _____

    _____

    d. _____

    _____

MORE BIBLICAL INSIGHTS ABOUT THE GIFTS

1. In 1 Peter 4:10 we find three very important principles regarding spiritual gifts. What are they?

    a. _use whatever ever gift you received_

    b. _faithfully administering God's grace_

    c. _____

2. What is a steward? (See 1 Peter 4:10.) Give a modern-day example.

    _____

    _____

    a. Does a steward own that with which he works? What implications does your answer hold for your understanding of a spiritual gift?_____

    _____

    _____

    b. What character qualities would you look for if you were going to hire a steward?_____

    _____

    c. What is a steward's main responsibility according to 1 Corinthians 4:2, and how does this responsibility apply to the believer's spiritual gift? _if your_ _gift is trust you must prove_ _faithfully_

3. What is Peter expressing in 1 Peter 4:11 about the exercise of the believer's gift? _use the strength_ _God provides so that God may be_ _praised through Jesus Christ_

39

a. How does one accomplish this goal: "that God may be glorified through Jesus Christ"? *the Spirit*
Ephesians 5:18 *Do not get drunk - be filled with*
1 Peter 2:12_____
1 John 1:9_____
b. What tendency in man is Peter warning the believer about in verse 11? *abstent from sinful desires*

4. What does Romans 11:29 add to our understanding about God and his relationship to spiritual gifts?_____ *his gifts are irrevocable*

5. There are other "grace gifts" from God mentioned in the New Testament which are not in the same category as the special spiritual gifts given to the church. Note them from the Scriptures below.
a. Romans 5:15, 16; 6:23_____
b. 1 Corinthians 7:7_____
c. 2 Corinthians 8:8–11 _____
_____

6. What stern warning does Paul give to Timothy in 1 Timothy 4:14 regarding his gift? *do not neglect your gift*
Why is it important to heed this warning? (See Luke 12:35-48.)_____
_____

7. Read 2 Timothy 1:3-11. What encouragement does Paul give Timothy in verse 6 that we should remember too?__ *fan into the flame the gift of God, which is in you*

THE GIFTS WORKING TOGETHER IN THE CHURCH
1. In 1 Corinthians 12:7 it says that the whole church profits when each believer is properly using his gift. How does the church profit?_____

2. Give a summary statement of what Paul is expressing in 1 Corinthians 12:20-25 with regard to gifts in the church.
_____
_____
_____

3. What does 1 Corinthians 12:26 tell us should be happening when gifted church members are all

ministering?_____

4. What are the two key goals for every church body as given in Ephesians 4:3? Explain what each phrase means in practical terms.

   a. _____
   _____

   b. _____
   _____

5. What is the crucial task given to the evangelists, pastors, and teachers according to Ephesians 4:12?_____

   a. In light of the above directive, do you think evangelists should be holding mass meetings around the world, or should they be involved in the local churches, training and teaching others to share their faith?_____
   _____

   b. Also, in light of the task given to pastors and teachers, should the church be hiring pastors and teachers to do the major share of the ministering? Why or why not?_____
   _____

   c. After the perfecting and ministry are progressing, what purpose do the gifts serve in the church? (See Ephesians 4:12c.)_____

6. What end goals are desired for every church member when the gifted believers are ministering to one another? (See Ephesians 4:13-17.)

   a. _____
   b. _____
   c. _____
   d. _____
   e. _____
   f. _____

7. Can the goals of verse 13 ever be realized in this life, or is Paul setting forth a utopian ideal never attainable this side of heaven? Explain your answer, using Ephesians 3:19; Colossians 1:9-11; 2:6, 7; Philippians 1:9-11.

_____

_____

_____

8. What emphasis will need to be supplied in the gifted church to insure that there will be no "tossed children" as noted in Ephesians 4:14; Hebrews 5:12—6:2?_____

_____

9. What principle regarding the gifts in their relationship to the local church can we derive from 1 Corinthians 1:7?

_____

_____

SIX
Evaluation One:
Your Spiritual Interests

How can you recognize your spiritual gift? As a Christian, your thoughts, preferences, attitudes, emotional reactions, and past and present service experiences will probably indicate your spiritual gift. By analyzing the exact makeup of these indicators, you can obtain insight that will help you determine your gift.

The greatest difficulty in forming an evaluation method is in trying to construct a procedure that will indicate your spiritual preferences and motivations rather than merely your natural talents and abilities. Because of the complexity of this challenge, no single evaluation or group of evaluations will indicate your gift. You can confirm any tentative conclusions only by actually serving. Therefore, the following evaluations are simply to help you narrow down the number of gifts you will need to test through serving.

PERSONAL ASSESSMENT
OF PREFERENCES AND TENDENCIES
Instructions:
  A. Circle as many answers to each question as solidly apply to you. DO NOT LIMIT YOUR RESPONSE TO ONE CHOICE if more than one applies, unless a specific limitation is given along with the question.
  B. Circle no response if you find that none of the choices apply to you. For example, if you prefer not to speak or make presentations, do not circle any of the answers in question 4.
    1. I prefer situations in my church in which I am:
       a. a speaker
       b. in a discussion group
       c. just a listener
    2. If asked to speak, I prefer to speak to:
       a. large groups
       b. small groups
       c. individuals
    3. When faced with counseling another person about his or her problems, I tend to:
       a. identify deeply with that person's situation

43

b. offer the best biblical solution I can think of, even if I'm not totally confident about my counsel

c. prefer sharing biblical insights, while avoiding discussions about feelings

d. urge him/her to follow my counsel, because I honestly believe God often helps me see solutions to others' problems

4. When I begin to prepare to speak to other Christians, I am normally motivated to:

a. emphasize the truths of basic Bible themes so as to lead the listeners to a clear-cut decision in the meeting

b. carefully organize a biblical passage in a systematic way so that the listeners can clearly understand its meaning

c. instruct on doctrinal topics to enable the listeners to have a better understanding of these subject areas

d. stress application of passages that emphasize practical truths, so that the listener's conduct can be refined

e. take one verse, and outline practical, specific steps of action for the listeners to follow

5. When listening to others speak, I tend to:

a. dislike in-depth doctrinal studies without applications

b. dislike talks which heavily emphasize illustrations and applications, without logical order and doctrine.

c. be strongly impressed by exhortations to serve other Christians

6. If I had to choose between the following approaches to personal devotions, I most prefer to (choose only one response):

a. search out how the verses I'm studying add to my understanding of doctrine

b. analyze the verses with the purpose of changing specific areas of my conduct

c. relate to the verses emotionally, so as to get a personal blessing

7. If I had my choice of passages to study, I would

usually choose ones which (choose only one response):

a. are rich in doctrine

b. are very practical

c. are controversial or difficult to understand

d. have great emotional appeal to my Christian life

8. When I give a testimony, I tend to:

a. encourage or console others, rather than just share a verse or experience

b. indicate some area of doctrine that has come alive to me through an experience and/or verse I've studied

c. emphasize the practical applications of some verses to my life

9. With regard to planning for the future of my church, I tend to:

a. have positive confidence about what the church should do

b. be concerned about and willing to do detailed, deliberate work on the plans

c. be more concerned with envisioning end results than with the details involved in getting there

d. have a great desire to see quick growth in the ministries of the church

10. When conversing with other Christians, I tend to:

a. probe them to determine their true spiritual condition and needs

b. exhort them to embrace certain goals and actions

11. If a person were to ask me to evaluate his or her spiritual condition, I would tend to:

a. point out errors in his or her mental understanding of the Christian life and doctrine

b. sense areas of right and wrong conduct in that person's life, and point out some solutions

c. be critical of areas of the person's life which are not disciplined and well ordered

12. When presented with a physical or spiritual need, I tend to:

a. respond on my own initiative to try to meet it if possible

45

b. respond best if someone calls and asks me to help fill it

c. not respond if the need requires considerable personal preparation

d. not respond if the need involves a lot of organizational detail and red tape

e. respond with money and possessions

13. In an organization, I usually prefer to (choose only one response):

a. lead a group

b. be a follower under another's leadership

14. When given a task which needs to be done now, I:

a. tend to complete it before taking on another task

b. tend to leave it for another task if the second one seems more important at the time

c. prefer to be told by a competent leader exactly what to do

d. tend to be concerned with doing a high quality and thorough job

e. favor doing it myself rather than delegating it

15. If asked to lead in a church program somewhere, I would tend to choose a position which involves:

a. comprehensive planning for the future

b. detailed planning and decision making for the present

c. harmonizing various viewpoints for a decision

d. evaluating personnel for various leadership positions

e. drawing up procedures and guidelines for effective inner working of the church

f. delegating responsibilities to others

16. If a group is meeting and no assigned leader is there, I would tend to:

a. assume the leadership

b. let the meeting proceed with no direct leadership

c. appoint or ask someone in the group to lead

d. call someone to find out who the real leader is

17. My reaction to the needs of others tends to be:

a. slow, because I don't know what to do

b. quick, because I sense what needs to be done most of the time

—c. deliberate, because I want to make sure I've
   thought it through thoroughly
18. In regard to decision making when the facts are
   clear, I tend to:
   —a. make decisions easily and with confidence
   —b. lack firmness because of people's feelings
   c. rely on others whom I believe are more capable
      of sorting out the issues in the decision
19. With regard to financial matters, I tend to:
   a. be able to make wise investments and gain
      wealth
   —b. be moved to give all I can to people and
      organizations I consider worthy
   c. want assurances that the money I give will be
      used wisely
   d. feel deeply that such matters should be handled
      in an orderly and prudent manner
   e. see money as a means for carrying out
      ministries and meeting needs, more than for
      construction of buildings, payment of salaries,
      etc.
   f. work hard to meet legitimate needs

20. If given a choice among the following
   involvements in a Sunday school class lesson, I
   would most favor (choose only one response):
   a. doing the biblical research and study to provide
      the lesson content
   —b. organizing available content and illustrations
      for presentation of the truths
   c. thinking up original applications for the lesson
      after having been given the organized content
   d. presenting the lesson for which the content,
      illustrations, and applications are provided

21. With regard to decisions made from my speaking,
   I prefer to (choose only one response):
   a. see an immediate commitment at the meeting
      by individuals in the group
   b. do follow-up counseling directed at long-run
      changes in conduct
   c. have an opportunity to explore the decision in
      depth through discussion
22. If I were a leader faced with two Christians in the

church who couldn't get along, I would tend to (choose only one response):

    a. change one person's responsibilities and position at the point of conflict

   —*b.* talk to the two people about changing their attitudes

    c. leave the situation alone, for fear of offending and making it worse

23. When called upon to serve, I am most naturally motivated to help in situations in which there are specific:

  —*a.* material needs (food, buildings, equipment, money)

    b. mental needs (lack of understanding of Scripture, need to find God's will in a certain matter, etc.)

    c. emotional needs (fear, anxiety, frustration, moods due to pain and trials, etc.)

    d. spiritual needs (for commitment, faith, dealing with sin, etc.)

24. When speaking before people, I:

    a. sense an inner urgency to persuade people to make spiritual decisions and commitments right then

    b. find it easy to accept the authority of the Scriptures without hesitation

  —*c.* am inwardly compelled to prepare well and speak carefully

    d. encourage thought-life decisions more than conduct changes

    e. feel most comfortable presenting a thorough, detailed study of a biblical passage or topic

    f. have an inner urge to share practical insights consistent with high biblical standards

    g. have a tendency to feel real concern for those in difficulty, and to suggest ways to help them

25. Generally speaking, I have a tendency to:

    a. visualize future goals and work toward them in spite of the difficulties

    b. be wise in discerning the character quality of another person

    c. accurately detect weaknesses and pitfalls when evaluating opportunities and situations *d.* have great energy and stamina for working on and meeting the practical needs of others

e. be sensitive to overall organizational direction more than minority, individual opinions

f. help meet obvious needs without measuring the worthiness of the recipient or evaluating his real needs

g. desire positive results and high quality in the things to which I give my efforts and money

h. see through others' actions to their real motives and inner attitudes

SCORE SHEET FOR PERSONAL ASSESSMENT OF PREFERENCES AND TENDENCIES

Instructions:

1. In the far left-hand column of this score sheet is a list of all the possible responses for the multiple choice questionnaire (1a, 1b, 1c, etc.). Transfer the circled answers from your questionnaire to this score sheet by circling the number-letter of each answer in the left-hand column that you circled in the questionnaire.

2. Each circled answer indicates an element of preference for one or more spiritual gifts. The spiritual gifts preferred by a given answer are indicated by an X in the boxes to the right of the response. For example, if you circled the answer 1a in the questionnaire, it indicates that you prefer preaching, teaching, and ruling, since the X's in the boxes to the right of 1a fall in the columns for those gifts.

3. Circle every X that you see as you move from the circled answers at the left across the page to your right. Do this for each circled response in the left-hand column.

4. Now, go to the end of the score sheet and notice that you must enter the total number of circled X's for each gift. To do this, count the circled X's in each gift column and enter the total in the box provided.

5. Then, go to the percentage equivalent chart at the end of the score sheet. Find the percentage equivalent to the number circled and enter it in the "% CIRCLED" box below the "TOTAL CIRCLED" box.

6. The top three or four percentages will indicate the gifts toward which you seem to show the greatest preference and tendency. List those gifts in order, starting with the one(s) with the highest percentage, on page 98, under 1.

7. See Appendix III if you have difficulty scoring the questionnaire.

	PREACHING	TEACHING	KNOWLEDGE	WISDOM	EXHORTATION	FAITH	DISCERNMENT OF SPIRITS	HELPS	SERVING	ADMINISTRATION	RULING	MERCY	GIVING
1a	X	X									X		
1b		(X)	(X)	(X)	(X)	(X)	(X)			(X)			
1c												(X)	
2a	X	X			X								
2b		X	X	X		X	X			X			
2c				X				X				X	
3a					X			X	X			X	X
3b	X	X				X					X	X	
3c			X										
3d					X	X		X					
4a	X												
4b		X											
4c			X										
4d				X									
4e					X								
5a					X	X		X	X				X
5b		X	X								X	X	
5c								X	X				X
6a		X	X										
6b					X	X		X					
6c	X					X		X	X			X	X
7a		X	X										
7b	X			X	X	X		X	X			X	X
7c		X	X				X						
7d	X											X	
8a					X	X						X	
8b	X	X	X										
8c	X			X				X	X	X			

50

PREACHING	TEACHING	KNOWLEDGE	WISDOM	EXHORTATION	FAITH	DISCERNMENT OF SPIRITS	HELPS	SERVING	ADMINISTRATION	RULING	MERCY	GIVING	
					X								9a
									X				9b
			X										9c
			X										9d
						X							10a
				X	X								10b
													10c
X	X	X											11a
				X		X							11b
									X	X			11c
								X				X	12a
							X						12b
							X						12c
							X	X					12d
												X	12e
X								X	X	X			13a
							X				X		13b
									X	X			14a
							X						14b
							X						14c
							X	X	X				14d
							X	X			X	X	14e
					X								15a
									X				15b
									X	X			15c
						X							15d
									X				15e
										X			15f
								X		X			16a
							X						16b
									X				16c
			X										16d
		X											17a
				X	X			X			X	X	17b
		X				X			X	X			17c
						X			X	X			18a
											X		18b

	PREACHING	TEACHING	KNOWLEDGE	WISDOM	EXHORTATION	FAITH	DISCERNMENT OF SPIRITS	HELPS	SERVING	ADMINISTRATION	RULING	MERCY	GIVING
18c								X					
19a													X
19b													X
19c													X
19d										X	X		X
19e					X								
19f													X
20a			X										
20b		X											
20c					X								
20d	X												
21a	X					X							
21b				X	X								
21c		X	X				X						
22a										X	X		
22b				X	X								
22c												X	
23a								X	X	X	X		X
23b		X	X	X									
23c					X							X	
23d	X					X	X						
24a	X												
24b	X												
24c		X											
24d		X											
24e		X											
24f				X									
24g					X								
25a						X							
25b							X						
25c							X						
25d									X				
25e											X		
25f												X	
25g													X
25h							X						

	PREACHING	TEACHING	KNOWLEDGE	WISDOM	EXHORTATION	FAITH	DISCERNMENT OF SPIRITS	HELPS	SERVING	ADMINISTRATION	RULING	MERCY	GIVING
TOTAL CIRCLED	2	4	2	6	7	5	5	8	8	8	6	9	8
% CIRCLED	13	25	13	38	44	31	31	50	50	50	38	56	50

	Total Circled	%	Total Circled	%
PERCENTAGES	1	6	9	56
	2	13	10	63
	3	19	11	69
	4	25	12	75
	5	31	13	81
	6	38	14	88
	7	44	15	94
	8	50	16	100

NOTE: If your results are the same or similar for three or four gifts, go to Appendix IV for evaluation of the results.

SEVEN
Evaluation Two:
Computerized Spiritual
Gifts Inventory (SGI)

The evaluation questionnaire in chapter six was brief and therefore, relatively easy to complete and score. The SGI in this chapter is more involved. However, the information gained is also far more extensive and detailed. By utilizing a specially designed computer program to evaluate your answers, you will have a range of helpful information at your disposal. Many people have found the additional insights well worth the time and cost.

The SGI evaluates your tendency toward only twelve spiritual gifts, rather than the thirteen we have been studying. The author of the SGI believes that the gift of helps and the gift of serving are actually *one gift* with two different names appearing in two separate Bible passages. Adjust your final conclusions about your gifts accordingly after you take this inventory.

The SGI was developed over a three-year period by Gordon McMinn, who holds a Ph.D. in counseling, and is a committed Christian with a deep interest in people becoming productive in their service to their local churches. Dr. McMinn worked extensively on spiritual gifts study material developed by Dr. Earl Radmacher and Professor Loren Fischer of Western Baptist Seminary and formulated the test and scoring. Churches have been profitably using the SGI since 1975. Dr. McMinn has graciously consented to release his rights to the inventory for inclusion in this book.

When you complete the inventory, mail it to:

Dr. Gordon McMinn
Route 2, Box 380
Forest Grove, Oregon 97116.

Your answers will be keypunched into a computer. The computer printout will be sent to you or to the designated leader or church if you are studying with a group.

The printout will provide several kinds of information. A chart will indicate how strongly you show preference toward each of the gifts. The same information will also be

THE SPIRITUAL GIFTS INVENTORY (MCMINN)

Please fill out the following information form:

☐ Dr.
☐ Mr.
☐ Mrs.
☐ Miss _____
      Name

_____
Street

_____
City   State   Zip

Telephone Number: Area Code (   ) _____

Marital Status:	**Educational Level:**	**Age:**
☐ Single	☐ High School or Less	☐ 11–20
☐ Married	☐ Two Years College	☐ 21–30
☐ Widowed	☐ College Graduate	☐ 31–40
☐ Divorced	☐ Professional Degree	☐ 41–50
	Specify _____	☐ 51–60
Sex:		☐ 61 & Over
☐ Male		
☐ Female		

Church Affiliation _____

Present Occupation _____

Comments _____

_____

_____

shown graphically, indicating positive and negative identification with each gift. Also, statements in the inventory about which you felt strongly, either positively or negatively, will be printed out for further consideration and discussion.

Finally, from your answers, some additional helpful insights will be given about the way you will tend to approach and carry out your service. For example, the printout will note if you prefer short-term or long-term projects and whether you like thinking work or physical work. The SGI records are retained in computer storage for a minimal period of one year, in case duplicate results are requested.

The costs involved in generating, handling, and mailing the computer printout are as follows:

Individual rate $10.00 per SGI
Group Rate for more than 10 SGI's $7.50 per SGI

Make your check or money order payable to Gordon McMinn and send it with the completed inventory to the above address. All orders must be prepaid.

Instructions:

1. In each triplet, please pencil an X in the square by the sentence which is "most" true and another X by the sentence which is "least" true about you. This means that the third statement would not have an X in front of it. Study the sample.

MOST LEAST

Sample: ☒ ☐ Enjoy a good steak dinner.
        ☐ ☐ Like to watch football on television.
        ☐ ☒ Fly on airplanes.

The sample indicates that you are a person who enjoys a good steak and that you are least likely to fly on airplanes.

Now do the practice triplet. Indicate which sentence is "most" like you and which is "least" like you, leaving one sentence blank.

MOST LEAST

Practice: ☐ ☐ Play the piano well.
         ☐ ☐ Dress sharply.
         ☐ ☐ Read a great deal of science fiction.

2. If you are taking this inventory for yourself, mentally insert the pronoun "I" before each sentence.
Example: I enjoy a good steak dinner.
3. If you are taking this inventory for someone else, mentally insert "Does he/she" before each sentence.
4. In many of the triplets that follow, you will find all three alternatives somewhat like you and perhaps none of them like you in other triplets. You must prioritize them anyway and say which is "most" like you out of the three alternatives and which is "least" like you out of the three alternatives.
5. It is not necessary to complete the inventory in one sitting. If you want to confer with others while you take it, that is acceptable. Don't take too long on any one triplet. Your first response is likely to be the most accurate.

1. ☐☐ Find it easy to pick out the main points in a presentation.
   ☐☐ Like to be told exactly what a job requires before accepting it.
   ☐☐ Seem to detect weak areas in a message more quickly than others.

2. ☐☐ Analyze a subject with care to get all the details.
   ☐☐ Tend to act on feelings without always thinking through the consequences.
   ☐☐ Talk with the designers to lay out plans for completion of a project.

3. ☐☐ Speak out to protect others when they are being misled.
   ☐☐ Match people with the right job and resources so the project goes smoothly.
   ☐☐ Take time to organize a talk so points will be clearly understood.

4. ☐☐ Work with people to help them complete a job after they start it.
   ☐☐ Like people to decide right away when the facts are known.
   ☐☐ Maintain an active interest in a topic even when study is tedious.

5. ☐☐ Get the job done even though many obstacles need to be overcome.
   ☐☐ Make decisions quickly but sometimes hold back due to uncertainty.
   ☐☐ Give up personal plans to let others have their way.

6. ☐☐ Use resources to assist people involved in loving deeds.
   ☐☐ Join in quickly to help others to get a job done.
   ☐☐ Accomplish almost any task if it is important for it to be done.

7. ☐☐ Find others who will join in to help people who are in need.
   ☐☐ Plan a project so that each worker has a defined responsibility.
   ☐☐ Seek out people to talk to who are well-informed on subjects.

8. ☐☐ Figure out what each person has to do to get the job done.
   ☐☐ Carefully follow plans developed by others.
   ☐☐ Sometimes neglect duties when caught up in a new idea.

9. ☐☐ Work hard to gain that which will benefit others.
   ☐☐ Confront people enthusiastically encouraging them to do their part.
   ☐☐ Suggest practical alternatives to people in perplexing situations.

10. ☐☐ Look for ways to be of service to others.
    ☐☐ Sense the hidden motives in why people act as they do.
    ☐☐ Work well with others as long as they do a good job.

11. ☐☐ Choose to be a worker rather than a leader on a project.
    ☐☐ Point it out to people when they have committed a sin.
    ☐☐ Tend to let other things slide to give full support to needy projects.

12. ☐☐ React strongly when resources are wasted.
    ☐☐ Guide the efforts of team members on a project.
    ☐☐ See that each member of the team does his or her part.

13. ☐☐ Look for practical ways to apply what is learned.
    ☐☐ Easily let go of one task to take on another one.
    ☐☐ Usually think of several options when helping someone make a decision.

14. ☐☐ Often contribute privately to needy causes when they are recognized.
    ☐☐ Develop a plan and recruit people so a project can be completed.
    ☐☐ Act to help people in need without thinking about the long-range effects.

15. ☐☐ Make efficient use of available resources.
    ☐☐ Occasionally go astray when following a hunch.
    ☐☐ Find it easy to accept what the Bible says without doubt.

16. ☐☐ Choose for friends those whose conduct is highly respected.
    ☐☐ Try to be very exact and get all the details when studying a topic.
    ☐☐ Seek to avoid recognition when contributing to a worthy cause.

17. ☐☐ Like to follow a plan without change once it has been accepted.
    ☐☐ Try new approaches confidently to achieve worthy goals.
    ☐☐ Tend to lose interest when projects are too long.

18. ☐☐ Give support to those in positions of leadership in the church.
    ☐☐ Find it easier to talk to a group than to an individual.
    ☐☐ Accept a job as the leader of a team rather than work alone.

19. ☐☐ Find it hard to accept people who don't live up to what they profess.
    ☐☐ Stick with a difficult assignment in spite of the obstacles.
    ☐☐ Quickly shift to try a new approach when an original plan does not work.

20. ☐☐ Think things through carefully before taking action.
    ☐☐ Easily find several alternatives to suggest to people facing decisions.
    ☐☐ Change from one project to another in order to get more done.

21. ☐☐ See that a job once started is carried through to completion.
    ☐☐ Have ability to piece together the details so as to see the full picture.
    ☐☐ Spend a lot of time thinking about new ideas.

22. ☐☐ Succeed in long-range investments.
    ☐☐ Trust people without listening carefully to what they say.
    ☐☐ Check to see if work is on schedule and according to plan.

23. ☐☐ Quickly spot a person who is insincere.
    ☐☐ Plan a course of action to utilize each resource efficiently.
    ☐☐ Usually read correctly what people are thinking or feeling.

24. ☐☐ Stay with people to encourage them to complete what they start.
    ☐☐ Catch on to what is happening more quickly than others do.
    ☐☐ Work patiently to achieve distant goals.

25. ☐☐ Follow up to see that people complete their assignments on a project.
    ☐☐ Quickly see through the motives of people.
    ☐☐ Deliberately plan speeches to encourage people to change.

26. ☐☐ Continually look for new ways to do a job better.
    ☐☐ Find it difficult to leave a task before it is finished.
    ☐☐ Risk being hurt to assist people to resolve their differences.

27. ☐☐ Readily accept exciting new ideas and try to implement them.
    ☐☐ Examine a biblical passage in view of its broader context.
    ☐☐ Find an urgency to speak to the basic needs of people.

28. ☐☐ Earnestly desire to explain biblical principles to people.
    ☐☐ Develop careful plans before starting on a project.
    ☐☐ Find it hard to ignore people who are in need.

29. ☐☐ Try to think through most problems in a logical, scientific way.
    ☐☐ Stay with a course of action in spite of obstacles.
    ☐☐ Find it irritating when people have not prepared adequately for a talk.

30. ☐☐ Check the consequences of each alternative before finalizing a decision.
    ☐☐ Take on any task when convinced of its worth.
    ☐☐ Carry through plans in spite of adversity.

31. ☐☐ Look forward to opportunities to talk with people.
    ☐☐ Take charge of a project assigning to each person what he should do.
    ☐☐ Readily do what those in positions of leadership ask to be done.

32. ☐☐ Talk to people about the importance of high standards of conduct.
    ☐☐ Find it difficult to work with people who are careless in what they do.
    ☐☐ Identify correctly the feelings of others.

33. ☐☐ Show leadership abilities in sticking to a plan.
    ☐☐ Feel at ease in talking with many different kinds of people.
    ☐☐ Prefer to speak to a group of people than to talk one-on-one.

34. ☐☐ Enlist people in order to accomplish planned goals.
    ☐☐ Confer with others to develop a good strategy for doing a job.
    ☐☐ Assist in jobs whether large or small.

35. ☐☐ Refuse to give up in spite of difficulties when working on a project.
    ☐☐ Seek to support activities which merit assistance.
    ☐☐ Point out to people in a tactful way changes they need to make.

36. ☐☐ Assume full responsibility to see that things get done.
    ☐☐ Find it easy to accept biblical data without question.
    ☐☐ Lay aside personal plans or desires to help others.

37. ☐☐ Get involved quickly to assist other team members on a project.
    ☐☐ Find a job in the project for every participant.
    ☐☐ Aim for a standard of excellence in all endeavors.

38. ☐☐ Prefer to work on short-range projects.
    ☐☐ Often continue to study after others quit to gain additional data.
    ☐☐ Understand complex ideas quickly.

39. ☐☐ Choose words carefully so as to explain ideas well.
    ☐☐ Enlist the efforts of all team members to complete a task.
    ☐☐ Welcome criticism but only change direction if fully persuaded.

40. ☐☐ Quickly spot the biblical principles when studying Scripture.
    ☐☐ Want people to respond in very practical ways to a message.
    ☐☐ Confer with leaders to develop an organizational plan.

41. ☐☐ Tend to hold to a viewpoint even when evidence is not very strong.
    ☐☐ Think through problems in a logical, scientific way.
    ☐☐ Want to share personal resources to see good things accomplished.

42. ☐☐ Rely heavily on intuitive ability.
    ☐☐ Persuade others to join in order to reach a goal.
    ☐☐ Explain the teachings of the Bible clearly and concisely.

43. ☐☐ Work hard to aid people who are worthy of assistance.
☐☐ Seem to be the first to speak out when others are being misled.
☐☐ Encourage people to do more so more can be accomplished.

44. ☐☐ Like a job where what needs to be done is stated in detail.
☐☐ See that each person does his or her share when working on a project.
☐☐ Persist when the going gets tough without getting upset.

45. ☐☐ Often respond to the need of others without thinking through the consequences.
☐☐ Make decisions and initiate action quickly.
☐☐ Confront people when they are doing wrong.

46. ☐☐ Present personal viewpoint on a subject only after careful study.
☐☐ Enjoy the challenge of seemingly impossible tasks.
☐☐ Accept personal hurt rather than risk offending someone.

47. ☐☐ Usually succeed in whatever task is undertaken.
☐☐ Display a cheerful spirit most of the time.
☐☐ Speak to people firmly when they fail to do their part on a job.

48. ☐☐ Stick to a project until the last detail is completed.
☐☐ Work hard though sometimes inwardly discouraged.
☐☐ Assume major responsibilities when asked in order to learn new skills.

49. ☐☐ Back up concerns with a personal investment.
☐☐ Frequently explain to people that the Bible sets a high standard for conduct.
☐☐ Divide responsibilities among others to get the task completed.

50. ☐☐ Usually rely on personal insight to know if people are being deceptive.
☐☐ Set timelines and job responsibilities to see a job gets done.
☐☐ Refuse to be discouraged even when things go wrong.

51. ☐☐ Enjoy making detailed, scholarly presentations.
☐☐ Choose for friends those who hold high standards of conduct.
☐☐ Work with others to develop a well-planned course of action.

52. ☐☐ Find it easy to talk to people though sometimes get too involved by doing so.
☐☐ Volunteer to help others when they need assistance.
☐☐ Ask others to participate in worthwhile activities.

53. ☐☐ Choose to work only on jobs where what is expected is stated clearly.
☐☐ Pick out informative details in study which others have not seen.
☐☐ Challenge people to take on more to accomplish what needs to be done.

54. ☐☐ Seek to be consistent in all dealing with people.
☐☐ Express personal viewpoint only after a careful study has been made.
☐☐ Stay away from people who appear to be hypocritical.

55. ☐☐ Spend extra effort to gain best long-range results.
☐☐ Want people to respond quickly when they hear the alternatives.
☐☐ Follow a plan carefully after a project has been clearly defined.

56. ☐☐ Decide quickly, yet cautiously.
☐☐ Work out strategies to help people solve their problems.
☐☐ Speak forcefully to get people to change from doing wrong to doing right.

57. ☐☐ Get frustrated when well-developed plans are changed impulsively.
    ☐☐ Want objectives to be clearly stated before supporting a project.
    ☐☐ Sometimes take on new projects without realizing how much is involved.

58. ☐☐ Like to study just for the purpose of gaining new information.
    ☐☐ Tend to take on new endeavors without realizing how much is involved.
    ☐☐ See to it that any job undertaken is done right.

59. ☐☐ Find it difficult to accept help from others.
    ☐☐ Speak up quickly when people overlook details in a Bible study.
    ☐☐ Sometimes get too deeply involved in the problems of others.

60. ☐☐ Work to get the most out of available resources.
    ☐☐ Have an ability to explain difficult portions of Scripture clearly.
    ☐☐ Sometimes permit emotions to cloud sound thinking.

61. ☐☐ Tend to be more confrontive with others than most people are.
    ☐☐ Focus on the information during a talk more than on the individual.
    ☐☐ Watch to see if people use what resources they have wisely.

62. ☐☐ Sometimes get too involved in the difficulties of others.
    ☐☐ Prefer doing the work on a job rather than planning for it.
    ☐☐ Help people who are in trouble to see some practical alternatives.

63. ☐☐ Need to know that efforts are accomplishing something worthwhile.
    ☐☐ Find ways to put many ideas into practice.
    ☐☐ Usually contribute only after factual data is provided to support the need.

64. ☐☐ Set up schedules in order to be consistent.
    ☐☐ Readily assume responsibility for supervising a job.
    ☐☐ Caution others about situations which may contain pitfalls.

65. ☐☐ Urge people to respond to a biblical message without delay.
    ☐☐ Take on assigned tasks readily whether large or small.
    ☐☐ Often support needy projects anonymously.

66. ☐☐ Possess a keen sensitivity to the needs of others.
    ☐☐ Encourage others to consider several alternatives before making a decision.
    ☐☐ Use a systematic approach to study the Bible.

67. ☐☐ Insist on adequate time to prepare before speaking.
    ☐☐ Take on difficult tasks without hesitating if endeavor is worthy.
    ☐☐ Prefer assignments with routine duties which are clearly outlined.

68. ☐☐ Guide the efforts of a team as opposed to working alone on projects.
    ☐☐ Prefer addressing a large group to a one-to-one discussion.
    ☐☐ Show great concern for the needs of people who are having problems.

69. ☐☐ Try to find all available data before coming to a conclusion.
    ☐☐ Often see several workable approaches to help others with their problems.
    ☐☐ Prefer well-defined, routine duties to other kinds of work.

70. ☐☐ Quickly pick out the central thought when reading.
    ☐☐ Tend to believe people before evaluating the situation fully.
    ☐☐ Keep moving toward goals in spite of potential problems.

71. ☐☐ Look beyond the faults and shortcomings of people to aid them.
    ☐☐ Work to get all members of a project involved in doing their tasks.
    ☐☐ Talk easily and openly with many different kinds of people.

72. ☐☐ Hesitate to conclude a study until a complete picture is developed.
    ☐☐ Evaluate progress often to see if things are going as planned.
    ☐☐ Formulate opinions quickly with a high degree of accuracy.

73. ☐☐ Try in everything that is done to set a good example for others.
    ☐☐ Confront people when they are doing wrong.
    ☐☐ Trust personal insight to know if people are not what they claim to be.

74. ☐☐ Operate intuitively at times.
    ☐☐ Arrive at implications of Scripture with little difficulty.
    ☐☐ Do things without help instead of accepting assistance from others.

75. ☐☐ Develop a long-range plan to obtain the best results.
    ☐☐ Want to help people in need even though the facts are not known.
    ☐☐ Try to get people to complete a task once they have started it.

76. ☐☐ Tend to be critical of people who do not keep high standards of conduct.
    ☐☐ Use ability to persuade others to do those jobs that need to be done.
    ☐☐ Plan talks in such a way that people will feel the need to respond.

77. ☐☐ Use part of what is earned through hard work to help people who deserve it.
    ☐☐ Prepare material for a speech so all those who listen will understand clearly.
    ☐☐ Often get busy talking to people and forget other duties that need to be done.

78. ☐☐ Often use own resources to assist in worthy causes.
    ☐☐ Prefer a well-planned discussion to casual conversation.
    ☐☐ Get irritated when people are standing around on a job because of poor planning.

79. ☐☐ Take responsibility as a leader when a task needs to be done.
    ☐☐ Find it easy to talk with people individually or in groups.
    ☐☐ Prefer to speak to a group rather than talk to people individually.

80. ☐☐ Expect to be told exactly what a job requires.
    ☐☐ Let people know in a positive way when they are not doing their part on a job.
    ☐☐ Have the ability to say things so clearly that almost everyone understands.

81. ☐☐ Perceive motives behind an action which others might not detect.
    ☐☐ Usually dig for more information than can be used when studying.
    ☐☐ Welcome a difficult assignment as an opportunity to learn.

82. ☐☐ Insist upon thorough preparation before making a presentation.
    ☐☐ Prefer making decisions quickly rather than hesitating.
    ☐☐ Understand what makes people act as they do.

83. ☐☐ Accept people readily in spite of their shortcomings.
    ☐☐ Find it easier to talk to a group than to counsel one person.
    ☐☐ Use words to explain situations well.

84. ☐☐ Often, through study, discover informative details others have not found.
    ☐☐ Come up with a good idea to help people in a difficult situation.
    ☐☐ Accept responsibility to be the manager on a project if asked.

85. ☐☐ Sometimes protect others on a job by accepting blame for their mistakes.
    ☐☐ Have the skill to explain biblical truth clearly and concisely.
    ☐☐ Use financial abilities to plan for the best use of available resources.

86. ☐☐ Often approach a job in a new way in an effort to learn a new skill.
    ☐☐ Try to find a plan that will help people when they are in trouble.
    ☐☐ Tend to lose enthusiasm on jobs that take a long time.

87. ☐☐ Gladly contribute to a cause when the money is put to good use.
    ☐☐ Stay with a task even though inwardly discouraged.
    ☐☐ Feel it is necessary to finish an assignment once it is started.

88. ☐☐ Need to see results to stay interested in a project.
    ☐☐ Study the Bible systematically trying to bring in the total picture.
    ☐☐ Enjoy digging for facts to gain new information.

89. ☐☐ Feel free to suggest an alternate plan to the boss if it will work better.
    ☐☐ Usually discount a message if the speaker appears to be phony.
    ☐☐ Struggle through hurts and joys with others to help them.

90. ☐☐ Study a matter carefully before expressing an opinion.
    ☐☐ Tend to get discouraged when a project goes on for a long time.
    ☐☐ Stick to an assignment until every detail is finished.

91. ☐☐ Like to contribute to special projects more than to routine programs.
    ☐☐ Have an ability to summarize a speech or an article clearly.
    ☐☐ Set the guidelines and procedures for the workers on a project.

92. ☐☐ Neglect own responsibilities at times to talk with people.
    ☐☐ Bring people and resources together so tasks can be done efficiently.
    ☐☐ Quickly spot the main points in a presentation.

93. ☐☐ Examine closely the worthiness of an endeavor before supporting it.
    ☐☐ Seek to set an example for others by being consistent in behavior.
    ☐☐ Assume responsibility to organize a work force for a project.

94. ☐☐ Like to explain the fine points of Scripture others often overlook.
    ☐☐ Tend to come to a conclusion too quickly.
    ☐☐ Remain optimistic even when difficulties are encountered.

95. ☐☐ Plan carefully so as to avoid waste in the use of supplies.
    ☐☐ Speak up quickly when others don't see details in Scripture.
    ☐☐ Readily see in daily activites how often biblical truth applies.

96. ☐☐ Feel the need to help people even though it is against better judgment.
    ☐☐ Skillfully point out to others what job needs to be done.
    ☐☐ Study carefully so as to pick up all the details.

97. ☐☐ Find new ways to do routine jobs to keep from getting bored.
    ☐☐ Encourage others to contribute by giving to worthy causes.
    ☐☐ Feel that people who get into difficulty must get out themselves.

98. ☐☐ Stay on a course of action once it has been established.
    ☐☐ Respond quickly to help people who are in need.
    ☐☐ Often change routine activities to try to find a better way to do the job.

99. ☐☐ Look for ways to make it practical when studying.
    ☐☐ Emphasize basic values repeatedly when speaking.
    ☐☐ Tend to be critical of others or to question their motives.

100. ☐☐ Determine to carry on even though many difficulties may be encountered.
    ☐☐ Use personal insight to evaluate situations and to pinpoint difficulties.
    ☐☐ Like to work with other members of a team on a project.

101. ☐☐ Readily see the biblical applications for a text.
    ☐☐ Get work started by offering to accept responsibility.
    ☐☐ Find many personal experiences are guided by biblical principles.

102. ☐☐ Get caught up in new ideas to the neglect of daily tasks.
    ☐☐ Welcome difficulties as opportunities for growth.
    ☐☐ Tell people when they are not doing what is right.

103. ☐☐ Summarize a presentation quickly by picking out the main points.
    ☐☐ Work hard so as to be able to invest in worthy causes.
    ☐☐ Study matters thoroughly so as to locate information others overlook.

104. ☐☐ Suggest to the boss another way to do the job if it will work better.
    ☐☐ Find a lot of satisfaction in detailed study and research.
    ☐☐ Keep feelings inside rather than risk offending someone.

105. ☐☐ Quickly get involved in new projects that have merit.
    ☐☐ Criticize those whose conduct is not in line with biblical standards.
    ☐☐ Recruit people to implement plans that have been developed.

106. ☐☐ Like to participate in panel discussions when panel members know their subject.
    ☐☐ React impatiently with those who repeatedly get into difficulty.
    ☐☐ Try to get people to reconcile their differences.

107. ☐☐ Need to be told when a job is done well.
    ☐☐ Tell people what changes they should make without offending them.
    ☐☐ Supervise a job to see that all the details are running smoothly.

108. ☐☐ Seem to have an ability to put people where they are most productive on a job.
    ☐☐ Sometimes defend a position even though confidence is lacking.
    ☐☐ Look for the best in people without doubting them.

109. ☐☐ Express an opinion to the leader if another way works better.
    ☐☐ Try to treat everyone the same way.
    ☐☐ Need to be reminded of the value of a project to stay involved.

110. ☐☐ Like to visit with people individually or in groups.
    ☐☐ Choose to discuss matters only with people who are well informed.
    ☐☐ Desire the best for people in spite of their faults.

111. ☐☐ Invest in projects only when convinced of their merit.
    ☐☐ Consciously try in all that is done to set an example of good behavior.
    ☐☐ Encourage people to keep growing in their Christian faith.

112. ☐☐ Find it difficult to refuse anyone who asks for aid.
    ☐☐ Enjoy study and want to learn as much as possible.
    ☐☐ Seek to find ways to put what is heard into practice.

MOST LEAST

113. ☐☐ Tell others when they need to change without offending them.
     ☐☐ Try to keep peace by avoiding controversial matters.
     ☐☐ Set a good example of behavior which is respected by others.

114. ☐☐ Reject emotional appeals for help unless facts are furnished to support the need.
     ☐☐ Find it hard to say no when asked to help others.
     ☐☐ Accept responsibility to oversee a project until it is completely finished.

115. ☐☐ Resist making decisions before carefully thinking through the consequences.
     ☐☐ Assume responsibility to get people started on a project.
     ☐☐ Feel uncomfortable when not thoroughly prepared to speak.

116. ☐☐ Refuse to give up on a task in spite of difficulties.
     ☐☐ Point out the weak spots to protect others from ideas which are misleading.
     ☐☐ Help people to take the next step in their Christian growth.

117. ☐☐ Capably direct a project when asked to assume that responsibility.
     ☐☐ Challenge people to do more so more good can be achieved.
     ☐☐ Use personal enthusiasm to get people to work harder.

118. ☐☐ At times argue a point even though not fully convinced.
     ☐☐ Detect where there may be problems when evaluating a proposal.
     ☐☐ Get irritated when people give a speech without adequate preparation.

119. ☐☐ Stick to goals in spite of adverse circumstances.
     ☐☐ Work on a plan to help people get out of their difficulties.
     ☐☐ Quickly recognize if a person's intentions are good or bad.

120. ☐☐ Evaluate the quality of a presentation easily spotting the main points.
     ☐☐ Use enthusiasm to get people to do more work.
     ☐☐ Look for things to do to help others who need assistance.

121. ☐☐ Consciously try to determine what God would want in each task of the day.
     ☐☐ Think of creative alternatives when facing obstacles.
     ☐☐ Go along with what others want rather than start a controversy.

122. ☐☐ Plan carefully so as to avoid wasted effort.
     ☐☐ Quickly capture the meaning of a biblical passage.
     ☐☐ Invest wisely to provide for self and for others.

123. ☐☐ Somehow find a way to accomplish a job if it's important.
     ☐☐ Feel deep concern for people who are going through difficulties.
     ☐☐ Set high goals for each undertaking.

124. ☐☐ Soon recognize when a person is being hypocritical.
     ☐☐ Stick to a job and work hard until it is finished.
     ☐☐ Set an example for others by supporting worthy endeavors.

125. ☐☐ Courageously move ahead even when others hesitate.
     ☐☐ Speak firmly to people at times in order to get work accomplished.
     ☐☐ Figure a way to get the most out of the resources that are available.

126. ☐☐ Point out to others what they could do to help finish a job.
     ☐☐ Find people who are willing to do a necessary assignment.
     ☐☐ Think of what biblical principles should be considered when making a decision.

127. ☐☐ Speak carefully on matters only after a careful study has been done.
☐☐ Patiently work with people no matter how difficult their situation.
☐☐ Persist, even work harder, though inwardly discouraged.

128. ☐☐ Hesitate to draw a conclusion until all the details have been studied.
☐☐ Accept the position as leader on a project to see each one does his or her job.
☐☐ Abandon personal plans or desires to let others have their way.

129. ☐☐ Volunteer to assist wherever abilities can be used.
☐☐ Engage in careful study so as not to overlook details.
☐☐ Lead out with new ideas which others can follow.

130. ☐☐ Discover ways whereby difficult tasks can be completed.
☐☐ Try to please people by responding in a way they expect.
☐☐ Talk people into making changes for the better.

131. ☐☐ Work to keep project on schedule by getting the most out of available resources.
☐☐ Remind people that their daily conduct should conform to what the Bible says.
☐☐ Work to help people settle their differences.

132. ☐☐ Take on what others consider to be impossible.
☐☐ Double own efforts when others fail to do their job.
☐☐ Recommend an alternate plan to the leader if it will work better.

133. ☐☐ Like to contribute when it can be seen that money is used for a good cause.
☐☐ Need frequent encouragement to stick with a long project.
☐☐ Take on any task with a determination to meet obstacles head on.

134. ☐☐ Readily accept what the Bible says without any question.
☐☐ Tend to stick with goals once they are established.
☐☐ Try to find biblical principles to serve as a guide for daily activities.

135. ☐☐ Maintain determination to accomplish tasks in spite of difficulties.
☐☐ Analyze most problems by using a logical or scientific method.
☐☐ Have a deep compassion and concern for people in their struggles.

136. ☐☐ Stop working on a project when beneficial results are no longer seen.
☐☐ Often repeat the primary truths of Scripture.
☐☐ Override people's opinions if necessary to do the job right.

137. ☐☐ Prefer to do a job than to give it to someone else to do.
☐☐ See how biblical principles are often worked out in daily experiences.
☐☐ Seem to be able to explain difficult portions of Scripture to others.

138. ☐☐ Answer questions and provide information with confidence.
☐☐ Encourage others to participate in worthwhile projects.
☐☐ Try to help people to settle their differences.

139. ☐☐ Like to stay with a project until it is completed in all of its details.
☐☐ Support those that are able to stretch their resources to get the most out of them.
☐☐ Discount the good if a person seems to say one thing and do another.

140. ☐☐ Evaluate situations and formulate accurate opinions quickly.
☐☐ See clearly even when many details cloud the main points.
☐☐ Risk being misunderstood to see that an important job gets done.

141. ☐☐ Like decisions to be made right away once people know the truth.
    ☐☐ Quickly see the total picture from examining the parts.
    ☐☐ Delay benefits now to gain more later.

142. ☐☐ Pick out biblical principles often overlooked by others.
    ☐☐ Tend to act quickly when presented with a challenge.
    ☐☐ Like to engage in a thorough analytic study of a topic.

143. ☐☐ Like to study topics in depth to develop a more complete picture.
    ☐☐ Explain to people how the Bible requires that they behave responsibly.
    ☐☐ Jump in quickly to help a person in a distressful situation.

144. ☐☐ Refuse to give up on others even when they fail.
    ☐☐ Invest wisely to achieve long-range goals.
    ☐☐ Feel an urgency to get jobs done without delay.

145. ☐☐ Assume responsibility to see the job gets done.
    ☐☐ Hold feelings of bitterness inside when people take advantage.
    ☐☐ Try to have a personal lifestyle which others can follow.

146. ☐☐ Tend to draw conclusions from outward appearances.
    ☐☐ Forego immediate returns in light of potential gain in the future.
    ☐☐ Study the Bible carefully to help people find practical applications.

147. ☐☐ Act quickly to help people when they need assistance.
    ☐☐ Speak up when what someone has said appears to be misleading others.
    ☐☐ Explain some alternatives to people who face difficult situations.

148. ☐☐ Talk more easily in a group setting than in a one-to-one setting.
    ☐☐ Use words well to express ideas.
    ☐☐ Get upset when people are wasteful with what they have.

149. ☐☐ Take the responsibility to see a job is done correctly.
    ☐☐ Often question the motives behind why a person did something.
    ☐☐ Think of several possibilities when helping a person make a decision.

150. ☐☐ Find a program of action to assist people with their difficulties.
    ☐☐ Often abandon personal plans to do what others want to do.
    ☐☐ Reserve opinion until carefully thought through.

151. ☐☐ Find it difficult to quit after a project is underway.
    ☐☐ Expect to see results when supporting a project.
    ☐☐ Set an example which others often follow.

152. ☐☐ Enjoy group interaction more than personal discussion.
    ☐☐ Look closely at new programs to see if they make wise use of their resources.
    ☐☐ Feel at ease in talking with groups or with individuals.

153. ☐☐ Decide carefully what to do in order to furnish a good example for others.
    ☐☐ Find social gatherings and games uninteresting.
    ☐☐ Put off routine duties when involved in a new project.

154. ☐☐ Use persuasive abilities effectively.
    ☐☐ Try to avoid controversial situations.
    ☐☐ Supervise others to see that the project gets completed.

155. ☐☐ Accept supervisory responsibility for all the details on a project.
      ☐☐ State the facts even though it may hurt the feelings of some people.
      ☐☐ Make a check to see if an appeal is legitimate before contributing.

156. ☐☐ Feel more comfortable talking to a group than to one person alone.
      ☐☐ Give full support to the decisions made by those in positions of leadership.
      ☐☐ Find it necessary to confront people sometimes to get things out in the open.

157. ☐☐ Try not to criticize people, but always look for the best in them.
      ☐☐ Feel an unusually strong concern for people who are going through a crisis.
      ☐☐ Help to pinpoint the source of a difficulty in a given situation.

158. ☐☐ Do the organizational work to get people started on a project.
      ☐☐ Tend to stay with the same job in a church rather than start a new one.
      ☐☐ Encourage people to grow through greater commitment to Christ.

159. ☐☐ Challenge people to live by biblical standards.
      ☐☐ Stay with a task and work hard until it is completed.
      ☐☐ Spend much time thinking about the needs of other people.

160. ☐☐ Do a good job of summarizing what someone has said or written.
      ☐☐ Challenge people to maintain good discipline in their lives.
      ☐☐ Find it very difficult to forgive people when they take advantage.

161. ☐☐ Feel confident in the ability to invest wisely.
      ☐☐ Stick firmly to a plan once it has been established.
      ☐☐ Study a biblical passage thoroughly so as not to overlook any details.

162. ☐☐ Assist others with a job until it is completely finished.
      ☐☐ Prefer organized discussions where participants have studied their subject.
      ☐☐ Usually understand why people feel as they do.

163. ☐☐ Join in quickly to assist other members of the team on a project.
      ☐☐ Look on the bright side of each situation.
      ☐☐ Use a logical, scientific method when approaching problems.

164. ☐☐ Often search for additional details before coming to a conclusion.
      ☐☐ Make decisions quickly unless some questions have created an uncertainty.
      ☐☐ Take time to determine the appropriate biblical principle before making a decision.

165. ☐☐ Seldom overlook details when studying.
      ☐☐ Quietly find a way to help meet the needs of others.
      ☐☐ Readily find biblical principles which pertain in making a decision.

166. ☐☐ Recognize when people are not what they claim to be.
      ☐☐ Rarely talk to people about deeply personal matters.
      ☐☐ Pick up details in such a way as to see the full picture readily.

167. ☐☐ Keep feelings inside rather than to take a chance of being misunderstood.
      ☐☐ Welcome the opportunity to invest in worthwhile endeavors.
      ☐☐ Find workable solutions to assist people who are in trouble.

168. ☐☐ Find details when studying which others have not discovered.
      ☐☐ Do practical things to help people when they need assistance.
      ☐☐ Present material in a well-organized way so that others understand.

169. ☐☐ Like to share personal resources to help people in worthy endeavors.
☐☐ Find it necessary to confront people when they fail to do their part on a job.
☐☐ Spot quickly where the difficulty is when evaluating a situation.

170. ☐☐ Tell people changes they need to make without alienating them.
☐☐ Take the initiative to organize a work force for a project.
☐☐ Try to protect others from being misled.

171. ☐☐ Delegate responsibilities to others easily.
☐☐ Seek new ways to do things to keep from getting bored.
☐☐ Understand the feelings and attitudes of many people.

172. ☐☐ Establish long-range objectives to gain the best results.
☐☐ Find ways to help people apply biblical truth to their daily activites.
☐☐ Prefer to engage in short-range as opposed to lengthy projects.

173. ☐☐ Feel bad about the troubles in which others find themselves.
☐☐ Look for the opportunity to share own resources with others.
☐☐ Have an ability to get people to work hard.

174. ☐☐ Talk with people to encourage them to do what needs to be done.
☐☐ Employ study skills when thinking about a topic to obtain precision.
☐☐ Consider any undertaking to be important.

175. ☐☐ Find it easy to get too involved when helping others.
☐☐ Stick to an assignment even though others have quit.
☐☐ Interpret Scripture with keen insight.

176. ☐☐ Invest time or resources only if need has been supported by factual data.
☐☐ Tend to be judgmental when people's motives are questionable.
☐☐ Study the Bible systematically trying to see how one part relates to another.

177. ☐☐ Accept the Bible and what it says without any question.
☐☐ Feel obligated to do a job rather than ask for assistance.
☐☐ Invest wisely to get the most out of available resources.

178. ☐☐ Make decisions quickly as a rule, but hesitate when uncertain.
☐☐ Seek assignments which are not too complicated.
☐☐ Deliberately plan talks to get observable results.

179. ☐☐ Quickly detect any hidden motives behind people's actions.
☐☐ Often act as mediator when people have disagreements.
☐☐ Have good success in delegating responsibilities to others.

180. ☐☐ Seek out well-informed people to get information on a subject.
☐☐ Easily put ideas into words which others readily understand.
☐☐ Try to do whatever is asked by the leaders in the church.

181. ☐☐ Usually sense when people are not what they claim to be.
☐☐ Take orders well but seldom assume leadership on a project.
☐☐ Stay with a job until it is finished once it has been started.

182. ☐☐ Refuse to be discouraged in spite of difficulties.
☐☐ Let other needs go sometimes when contributing to a very worthy cause.
☐☐ Avoid discussion with people on deeply personal matters.

183. ☐☐ Find own efforts of leadership respected by others.
     ☐☐ Try to think of what God would want done in all that is undertaken.
     ☐☐ Express a desire to keep present assignment when asked to consider a new one

184. ☐☐ Prefer to work as a leader on a team than to work alone.
     ☐☐ Like to engage in scholarly discussions with well-informed people.
     ☐☐ Listen carefully to criticism but resist change until fully persuaded.

185. ☐☐ Protect others from being taken by a sales pitch.
     ☐☐ Set a personal example of behavior which others have said they respect.
     ☐☐ Think the truth should be known even if feelings are hurt.

186. ☐☐ Like to work on projects but would rather not be the leader.
     ☐☐ Often hold feelings of guilt inside after being hurt by someone.
     ☐☐ Prefer to deal with facts rather than with feelings.

187. ☐☐ Feel confident to do a job when it needs to be done.
     ☐☐ Move ahead with great determination to achieve goals.
     ☐☐ Sometimes appear more confident than is really the case.

188. ☐☐ Tend to hold feelings inside if the other person appears insensitive.
     ☐☐ Look for difficult assignments in order to learn more.
     ☐☐ Stick with a job until it is completely finished.

189. ☐☐ Approach the future with confidence that goals will be achieved.
     ☐☐ Suggest practical ways to apply biblical principles.
     ☐☐ Encourage people to take action once they know the truth.

190. ☐☐ Sacrifice personal desires rather than risk offending someone.
     ☐☐ Look for different ways to do a job so as to learn new skills.
     ☐☐ Consistently endeavor to fulfill all responsibilities to others.

191. ☐☐ Lay out careful plans before starting a particular course of action.
     ☐☐ Often study just to gain more information on a subject.
     ☐☐ Tend to criticize others if their motives appear questionable.

192. ☐☐ Need to be told that work is appreciated and worthwhile.
     ☐☐ Set the pace for others when facing a challenge.
     ☐☐ Correct others when it is obvious they have made a mistake.

EIGHT
Evaluation Three:
Spiritual Interests
Others See in You

No person is totally objective about himself. His self-image affects his viewpoint about his natural talents. The same is true about his spiritual gifts. Therefore, it is helpful to have others participate in the determination of what our spiritual gifts are.

The following questionnaire should be filled in by the four Christians who know you best. One's parents and one's marriage partner should definitely be considered for this purpose. Then, choose others on the basis of the length of time they have known you, and the depth of your friendship with them.

After you have received the completed questionnaires and scored them, analyze the results to see whether any gifts appear to be predominant. Enter those gifts on page 99.

If the score sheet indicates that three or four gifts have the same or very similar percentages, go to Appendix V for help in evaluating the results.

OTHERS' ASSESSMENT
OF PREFERENCES AND TENDENCIES
Instructions:
   A. Circle as many answers to each question as solidly apply to the person you are evaluating. DO NOT LIMIT YOUR RESPONSE TO ONE CHOICE if more than one applies, unless a specific limitation is given along with the question.
   B. Circle no response if you find that none of the choices apply. For example, if you believe that the person prefers not to speak or make presentations, do not circle any of the answers in question 4.
      1. He/she prefers situations in the church in which he/she is:
         a. a speaker
         b. in a discussion group
         c. just a listener
      2. If asked to speak, he/she prefers to speak to:

a. large groups
b. small groups
c. individuals

3. When faced with counseling another person about problems, he/she tends to:
   a. identify deeply with the other person's situation
   b. give the other person the best biblical solution he/she can think of, even if not totally confident about the counsel
   c. prefer sharing biblical insights, avoiding discussions about feelings
   d. urge the person to follow his/her counsel, because he/she honestly believes God helps him/her see the solutions to others' problems

4. When preparing for talks to other Christians, he/she is normally motivated to:
   a. emphasize the truths of basic Bible themes, so as to lead the listeners to a clear-cut decision in the meeting
   b. carefully organize a biblical passage in a systematic way, so that the listeners clearly understand it
   c. instruct on doctrinal topics, to enable the listeners to have a better understanding of these subjects
   d. stress application of passages emphasizing practical truths, so that the listeners can refine their conduct
   e. take one verse and outline practical and specific steps of action for the listener to follow

5. When giving a testimony, he/she tends to:
   a. encourage or console others, rather than just share a verse or experience
   b. indicate some area of doctrine that has come alive through an experience or a shared verse
   c. emphasize the practical application of some verses to his or her life

6. With regard to planning for the future of his/her church, he/she tends to:
   a. have confidence about what the church should do
   b. be more concerned with envisioning end results than with the details involved in getting there

    c. have a great desire to see quick growth in the
       ministries of the church

7. When conversing with other Christians, he/she
   tends to:
    a. probe them to determine their true spiritual
       condition and needs
    b. exhort them to embrace certain goals and
       actions

8. If a person were to ask him/her to evaluate
   another's spiritual condition, he/she would tend to:
    a. point out errors in the other person's mental
       understanding of the Christian life
    b. sense areas of right and wrong conduct in that
       person's life, and point out some solutions
    c. be critical of areas of that person's life which
       are not disciplined and well ordered

9. When presented with a physical or spiritual need,
   he/she tends to:
    a. respond on his/her own initiative to try to meet
       it if possible
    b. respond best if someone calls and asks him/her
       to help
    c. not respond if the need requires some time for
       personal preparation
    d. respond with money and possessions

10. In an organization, he/she prefers to (choose only
    one response):
    a. lead a group
    b. be a follower under another's leadership

11. When given a task which needs to be done now,
    he/she tends to:
    a. leave it for another task if the second one
       seems more important at the time
    b. be concerned with doing a high quality and
       thorough job
    c. favor doing it himself/herself rather than
       delegating it

12. If asked to lead somewhere in the church
    program, he/she would tend to choose a position
    which involved:
    a. detailed planning and decision making for the
       present
    b. harmonizing various viewpoints for a decision

    c. evaluating personnel for various leadership positions

13. If a group is meeting and no assigned leader is there, he/she would tend to:
    a. assume the leadership
    b. let the meeting proceed with no direct leadership
    c. call someone to find out who the real leader is

14. His/her reaction to the needs of others tends to be:
    a. slow, because of not knowing what to do
    b. quick, because he/she usually senses what needs to be done
    c. deliberate, because of wanting to make sure he/she has thought it through thoroughly

15. In regard to decision making when the facts are clear, he/she tends to:
    a. lack firmness, because of people's feelings
    b. rely on others whom he/she believes are more capable of sorting out the issues in the decision

16. With regard to financial matters, he/she tends to:
    a. be able to make wise investments and gain wealth
    b. be moved to give generously to people and organizations he/she considers worthy
    c. feel deeply that such matters should be handled in an orderly and prudent manner
    d. see money as a means for carrying out ministries and meeting needs, more than for construction of buildings, payment of salaries, etc.
    e. work hard to meet legitimate needs

17. When called upon to serve, he/she is most naturally motivated to help in situations in which there are specific:
    a. material needs (food, buildings, equipment, money)
    b. mental needs (lack of understanding of Scripture, need to find God's will in a certain area, etc.)
    c. emotional needs (fear, anxiety, frustration, moods due to pain and trials, etc.)
    d. spiritual needs (for commitment, faith, dealing with sin, etc.)

18. When speaking before people, he/she has the tendency to:
   a. try to persuade people to make spiritual decisions and commitments right then
   b. prepare well and speak carefully
   c. encourage thought-life decisions more than conduct changes
   d. have little interest in emotional commitments unless they are based on clear biblical teaching

OTHERS' ASSESSMENT
OF PREFERENCES AND TENDENCIES
Instructions:
   A. Circle as many answers to each question as solidly apply to the person you are evaluating. DO NOT LIMIT YOUR RESPONSE TO ONE CHOICE if more than one applies, unless a specific limitation is given along with the question.
   B. Circle no response if you find that none of the choices apply. For example, if you believe that the person prefers not to speak or make presentations, do not circle any of the answers in question 4.
      1. He/she prefers situations in the church in which he/she is:
         a. a speaker
         b. in a discussion group
         c. just a listener
      2. If asked to speak, he/she prefers to speak to:
         a. large groups
         b. small groups
         c. individuals
      3. When faced with counseling another person about problems, he/she tends to:
         a. identify deeply with the other person's situation
         b. give the other person the best biblical solution he/she can think of, even if not totally confident about the counsel
         c. prefer sharing biblical insights, avoiding discussions about feelings
         d. urge the person to follow his/her counsel, because he/she honestly believes God helps him/her see the solutions to others' problems
      4. When preparing for talks to other Christians,

he/she is normally motivated to:

a. emphasize the truths of basic Bible themes, so as to lead the listeners to a clear-cut decision in the meeting

b. carefully organize a biblical passage in a systematic way, so that the listeners clearly understand it

c. instruct on doctrinal topics, to enable the listeners to have a better understanding of these subjects

d. stress application of passages emphasizing practical truths, so that the listeners can refine their conduct

e. take one verse and outline practical and specific steps of action for the listener to follow

5. When giving a testimony, he/she tends to:

a. encourage or console others, rather than just share a verse or experience

b. indicate some area of doctrine that has come alive to him or her through an experience or a shared verse

c. emphasize the practical application of some verses to his or her life

6. With regard to planning for the future of his/her church, he/she tends to:

a. have confidence about what the church should do

b. be more concerned with envisioning end results than with the details involved in getting there

c. have a great desire to see quick growth in the ministries of the church

7. When conversing with other Christians, he/she tends to:

a. probe them to determine their true spiritual condition and needs

b. exhort them to embrace certain goals and actions

8. If a person were to ask him/her to evaluate another's spiritual condition, he/she would tend to:

a. point out errors in the other person's mental understanding of the Christian life

b. sense areas of right and wrong conduct in that person's life, and point out some solutions

    c. be critical of areas of that person's life which
       are not disciplined and well ordered

9. When presented with a physical or spiritual need,
  he/she tends to:
    a. respond on his/her own initiative to try to meet
       it if possible
    b. respond best if someone calls and asks him/her
       to help
    c. not respond if the need requires some time for
       personal preparation
    d. respond with money and possessions

10. In an organization, he/she prefers to (choose only
  one response):
    a. lead a group
    b. be a follower under another's leadership

11. When given a task which needs to be done now,
  he/she tends to:
    a. leave it for another task if the second one
       seems more important at the time
    b. be concerned with doing a high quality and
       thorough job
    c. favor doing it himself/herself rather than
       delegating it

12. If asked to lead somewhere in the church
  program, he/she would tend to choose a position
  which involved:
    a. detailed planning and decision making for the
       present
    b. harmonizing various viewpoints for a decision
    c. evaluating personnel for various leadership
       positions

13. If a group is meeting and no assigned leader is
  there, he/she would tend to:
    a. assume the leadership
    b. let the meeting proceed with no direct
       leadership
    c. call someone to find out who the real leader is

14. His/her reaction to the needs of others tends to be:
    a. slow, because of not knowing what to do
    b. quick, because he/she usually senses what
       needs to be done
    c. deliberate, because of wanting to make sure
       he/she has thought it through thoroughly

15. In regard to decision making when the facts are clear, he/she tends to:
    a. lack firmness, because of people's feelings
    b. rely on others whom he/she believes are more capable of sorting out the issues in the decision
16. With regard to financial matters, he/she tends to:
    a. be able to make wise investments and gain wealth
    b. be moved to give generously to people and organizations he/she considers worthy
    c. feel deeply that such matters should be handled in an orderly and prudent manner
    d. see money as a means for carrying out ministries and meeting needs, more than for construction of buildings, payment of salaries, etc.
    e. work hard to meet legitimate needs
17. When called upon to serve, he/she is most naturally motivated to help in situations in which there are specific:
    a. material needs (food, buildings, equipment, money)
    b. mental needs (lack of understanding of Scripture, need to find God's will in a certain area, etc.)
    c. emotional needs (fear, anxiety, frustration, moods due to pain and trials, etc.)
    d. spiritual needs (for commitment, faith, dealing with sin, etc.)
18. When speaking before people, he/she has the tendency to:
    a. try to persuade people to make spiritual decisions and commitments right then
    b. prepare well and speak carefully
    c. encourage thought-life decisions more than conduct changes
    d. have little interest in emotional commitments unless they are based on clear biblical teaching

OTHERS' ASSESSMENT
OF PREFERENCES AND TENDENCIES
Instructions:
 A. Circle as many answers to each question as solidly

apply to the person you are evaluating. DO NOT LIMIT
YOUR RESPONSE TO ONE CHOICE if more than one applies,
unless a specific limitation is given along with the
question.

B. Circle no response if you find that none of the choices
apply. For example, if you believe that the person
prefers not to speak or make presentations, do not
circle any of the answers in question 4.

1. He/she prefers situations in the church in which
   he/she is:
   a. a speaker
   b. in a discussion group
   c. just a listener

2. If asked to speak, he/she prefers to speak to:
   a. large groups
   b. small groups
   c. individuals

3. When faced with counseling another person about
   problems, he/she tends to:
   a. identify deeply with the other person's situation
   b. give the other person the best biblical solution
      he/she can think of, even if not totally
      confident about the counsel
   c. prefer sharing biblical insights, avoiding
      discussions about feelings
   d. urge the person to follow his/her counsel,
      because he/she honestly believes God helps
      him/her see the solutions to others' problems

4. When preparing for talks to other Christians,
   he/she is normally motivated to:
   a. emphasize the truths of basic Bible themes, so
      as to lead the listeners to a clear-cut decision
      in the meeting
   b. carefully organize a biblical passage in a
      systematic way, so that the listeners clearly
      understand it
   c. instruct on doctrinal topics, to enable the
      listeners to have a better understanding of
      these subjects
   d. stress application of passages emphasizing
      practical truths, so that the listeners can refine
      their conduct

    e. take one verse and outline practical and
       specific steps of action for the listener to follow

5. When giving a testimony, he/she tends to:
    a. encourage or console others, rather than just
       share a verse or experience
    b. indicate some area of doctrine that has come
       alive to him/her through an experience or a
       shared verse
    c. emphasize the practical application of some
       verses to his or her life

6. With regard to planning for the future of his/her
   church, he/she tends to:
    a. have confidence about what the church should
       do
    b. be more concerned with envisioning end results
       than with the details involved in getting there
    c. have a great desire to see quick growth in the
       ministries of the church

7. When conversing with other Christians, he/she
   tends to:
    a. probe them to determine their true spiritual
       condition and needs
    b. exhort them to embrace certain goals and
       actions

8. If a person were to ask him/her to evaluate
   another's spiritual condition, he/she would tend to:
    a. point out errors in the other person's mental
       understanding of the Christian life
    b. sense areas of right and wrong conduct in that
       person's life, and point out some solutions
    c. be critical of areas of that person's life which
       are not disciplined and well ordered

9. When presented with a physical or spiritual need,
   he/she tends to:
    a. respond on his/her own initiative to try to meet
       it if possible
    b. respond best if someone calls and asks him/her
       to help
    c. not respond if the need requires some time for
       personal preparation
    d. respond with money and possessions

10. In an organization, he/she prefers to (choose only
    one response):

    a. lead a group

    b. be a follower under another's leadership

11. When given a task which needs to be done now, he/she tends to:

    a. leave it for another task if the second one seems more important at the time

    b. be concerned with doing a high quality and thorough job

    c. favor doing it himself/herself rather than delegating it

12. If asked to lead somewhere in the church program, he/she would tend to choose a position which involved:

    a. detailed planning and decision making for the present

    b. harmonizing various viewpoints for a decision

    c. evaluating personnel for various leadership positions

13. If a group is meeting and no assigned leader is there, he/she would tend to:

    a. assume the leadership

    b. let the meeting proceed with no direct leadership

    c. call someone to find out who the real leader is

14. His/her reaction to the needs of others tends to be:

    a. slow, because of not knowing what to do

    b. quick, because he/she usually senses what needs to be done

    c. deliberate, because of wanting to make sure he/she has thought it through thoroughly

15. In regard to decision making when the facts are clear, he/she tends to:

    a. lack firmness, because of people's feelings

    b. rely on others whom he/she believes are more capable of sorting out the issues in the decision

16. With regard to financial matters, he/she tends to:

    a. be able to make wise investments and gain wealth

    b. be moved to give generously to people and organizations he/she considers worthy

    c. feel deeply that such matters should be handled in an orderly and prudent manner

    d. see money as a means for carrying out

ministries and meeting needs, more than for
construction of buildings, payment of salaries,
etc.

    e. work hard to meet legitimate needs

17. When called upon to serve, he/she is most
naturally motivated to help in situations in which
there are specific:
    a. material needs (food, buildings, equipment,
    money)
    b. mental needs (lack of understanding of
    Scripture, need to find God's will in a certain
    area, etc.)
    c. emotional needs (fear, anxiety, frustration,
    moods due to pain and trials, etc.)
    d. spiritual needs (for commitment, faith, dealing
    with sin, etc.)

18. When speaking before people, he/she has the
tendency to:
    a. try to persuade people to make spiritual
    decisions and commitments right then
    b. prepare well and speak carefully
    c. encourage thought-life decisions more than
    conduct changes
    d. have little interest in emotional commitments
    unless they are based on clear biblical teaching

OTHERS' ASSESSMENT
OF PREFERENCES AND TENDENCIES

Instructions:

  A. Circle as many answers to each question as solidly
apply to the person you are evaluating. DO NOT LIMIT
YOUR RESPONSE TO ONE CHOICE if more than one applies,
unless a specific limitation is given along with the
question.

  B. Circle no response if you find that none of the choices
apply. For example, if you believe that the person
prefers not to speak or make presentations, do not
circle any of the answers in question 4.

    1. He/she prefers situations in the church in which
he/she is:
    a. a speaker
    b. in a discussion group
    c. just a listener

2. If asked to speak, he/she prefers to speak to:
   a. large groups
   b. small groups
   c. individuals
3. When faced with counseling another person about problems, he/she tends to:
   a. identify deeply with the other person's situation
   b. give the other person the best biblical solution he/she can think of, even if not totally confident about the counsel
   c. prefer sharing biblical insights, avoiding discussions about feelings
   d. urge the person to follow his/her counsel, because he/she honestly believes God helps him/her see the solutions to others' problems
4. When preparing for talks to other Christians, he/she is normally motivated to:
   a. emphasize the truths of basic Bible themes, so as to lead the listeners to a clear-cut decision in the meeting
   b. carefully organize a biblical passage in a systematic way, so that the listeners clearly understand it
   c. instruct on doctrinal topics, to enable the listeners to have a better understanding of these subjects
   d. stress application of passages emphasizing practical truths, so that the listeners can refine their conduct
   e. take one verse and outline practical and specific steps of action for the listener to follow
5. When giving a testimony, he/she tends to:
   a. encourage or console others, rather than just share a verse or experience
   b. indicate some area of doctrine that has come alive to him/her through an experience or a shared verse
   c. emphasize the practical application of some verses to his or her life
6. With regard to planning for the future of his/her church, he/she tends to:
   a. have confidence about what the church should do

    b. be more concerned with envisioning end results than with the details involved in getting there

    c. have a great desire to see quick growth in the ministries of the church

7. When conversing with other Christians, he/she tends to:

    a. probe them to determine their true spiritual condition and needs

    b. exhort them to embrace certain goals and actions

8. If a person were to ask him/her to evaluate another's spiritual condition, he/she would tend to:

    a. point out errors in the other person's mental understanding of the Christian life

    b. sense areas of right and wrong conduct in that person's life, and point out some solutions

    c. be critical of areas of that person's life which are not disciplined and well ordered

9. When presented with a physical or spiritual need, he/she tends to:

    a. respond on his/her own initiative to try to meet it if possible

    b. respond best if someone calls and asks him/her to help

    c. not respond if the need requires some time for personal preparation

    d. respond with money and possessions

10. In an organization, he/she prefers to (choose only one response):

    a. lead a group

    b. be a follower under another's leadership

11. When given a task which needs to be done now, he/she tends to:

    a. leave it for another task if the second one seems more important at the time

    b. be concerned with doing a high quality and thorough job

    c. favor doing it himself/herself rather than delegating it

12. If asked to lead somewhere in the church program, he/she would tend to choose a position which involved:

a. detailed planning and decision making for the present
b. harmonizing various viewpoints for a decision
c. evaluating personnel for various leadership positions

13. If a group is meeting and no assigned leader is there, he/she would tend to:
a. assume the leadership
b. let the meeting proceed with no direct leadership
c. call someone to find out who the real leader is

14. His/her reaction to the needs of others tends to be:
a. slow, because of not knowing what to do
b. quick, because he/she usually senses what needs to be done
c. deliberate, because of wanting to make sure he/she has thought it through thoroughly

15. In regard to decision making when the facts are clear, he/she tends to:
a. lack firmness, because of people's feelings
b. rely on others whom he/she believes are more capable of sorting out the issues in the decision

16. With regard to financial matters, he/she tends to:
a. be able to make wise investments and gain wealth
b. be moved to give generously to people and organizations he/she considers worthy
c. feel deeply that such matters should be handled in an orderly and prudent manner
d. see money as a means for carrying out ministries and meeting needs, more than for construction of buildings, payment of salaries, etc.
e. work hard to meet legitimate needs

17. When called upon to serve, he/she is most naturally motivated to help in situations in which there are specific:
a. material needs (food, buildings, equipment, money)
b. mental needs (lack of understanding of Scripture, need to find God's will in a certain area, etc.)
c. emotional needs (fear, anxiety, frustration, moods due to pain and trials, etc.)
d. spiritual needs (for commitment, faith, dealing with sin, etc.)

18. When speaking before people, he/she has the
tendency to:
   a. try to persuade people to make spiritual
      decisions and commitments right then
   b. prepare well and speak carefully
   c. encourage thought-life decisions more than
      conduct changes
   d. have little interest in emotional commitments
      unless they are based on clear biblical teaching

SCORE SHEET FOR OTHERS' ASSESSMENT OF PREFERENCES AND TENDENCIES

Instructions:
1. In the far left-hand column of this score sheet is a list
   of all the possible responses for the multiple choice
   questionnaire (1a, 1b, 1c, etc.). Transfer the circled
   answers from the questionnaire to this score sheet by
   circling each answer in the left-hand column that you
   find circled in the questionnaire.
2. Each circled answer indicates a preference for one or
   more spiritual gifts. The spiritual gifts preferred by a
   given answer are indicated by an X in the boxes to
   the right of the response. For example, if you find
   circled the answer 1a in the questionnaire, it
   indicates that you prefer preaching, teaching, and
   ruling, since the X's in the boxes to the right of 1a
   fall in the columns for those gifts.
3. Circle every X that you see as you move from the
   circled answers at the left across the page to your
   right. Do this for each circled response in the
   left-hand column.
4. Now, go to the end of the score sheet and notice that
   you must enter the total number of circled X's for
   each gift. To do this, count the circled X's in each gift
   column and enter the total in the box provided.
5. Then, go to the percentage equivalent chart at the
   end of the score sheet. Find the percentage equivalent
   to the number circled and enter it in the "% CIRCLED
   box" below the "TOTAL CIRCLED" box.
6. The top three or four percentages will indicate the
   gifts toward which you seem to show the greatest
   preference or tendency.
7. Follow the procedures 1—6 above for each of the four

questionnaires completed by others. Evaluate the four score sheets and enter the top three or four gifts on page 99, under 2.

8. See Appendix III if you have difficulty scoring the questionnaires.

	PREACHING	TEACHING	KNOWLEDGE	WISDOM	EXHORTATION	FAITH	DISCERNMENT OF SPIRITS	HELPS	SERVING	ADMINISTRATION	RULING	MERCY	GIVING
1a	X	X									X		
1b		X	X	X	X	X	X			X			
1c												X	
2a	X	X			X								
2b		X	X	X		X	X			X			
2c				X				X				X	
3a					X			X	X			X	X
3b	X	X				X					X	X	
3c			X										
3d				X	X		X						
4a	X												
4b		X											
4c			X										
4d				X									
4e					X								
5a				X	X							X	
5b	X	X	X										
5c	X			X			X	X	X				
6a						X							
6b						X							
6c						X							
7a							X						
7b					X	X							
8a	X	X	X										
8b				X			X						
8c										X	X		
9a									X				X
9b								X					
9c								X					

89

PREACHING	TEACHING	KNOWLEDGE	WISDOM	EXHORTATION	FAITH	DISCERNMENT OF SPIRITS	HELPS	SERVING	ADMINISTRATION	RULING	MERCY	GIVING	
												X	9
X								X	X	X			10a
						X					X		10b
								X					11a
								X	X	X			11b
							X	X			X	X	11c
									X				12a
									X	X			12b
						X							12c
								X		X			13a
							X						13b
			X										13c
		X											14a
				X	X			X			X	X	14b
			X			X			X	X			14c
											X		15a
							X						15b
												X	16a
												X	16b
									X	X		X	16c
				X									16d
												X	16e
							X	X	X	X		X	17a
	X	X	X										17b
				X							X		17c
X					X	X							17d
X													18a
	X												18b
			X										18c
			X										18d

TOTAL CIRCLED	2	4	3	6	4	5	5	6	5	7	4	5	6
% CIRCLED													

	Total Circled	%	Total Circled	%
	1	10	6	60
	2	20	7	70
	3	30	8	80
	4	40	9	90
	5	50	10	100

	PREACHING	TEACHING	KNOWLEDGE	WISDOM	EXHORTATION	FAITH	DISCERNMENT OF SPIRITS	HELPS	SERVING	ADMINISTRATION	RULING	MERCY	GIVING
1a	X	X									X		
1b		X	X	X	X	X	X			X			
1c												X	
2a	X	X			X								
2b		X	X	X		X	X			X			
2c				X				X				X	
3a					X			X	X			X	X
3b	X	X			X						X	X	
3c		X											
3d				X	X		X						
4a	X												
4b		X											
4c			X										
4d				X									
4e					X								
5a					X	X						X	
5b	X	X	X										
5c	X				X			X	X	X			
6a						X							
6b						X							
6c						X							
7a							X						
7b					X	X							
8a	X	X	X										
8b					X		X						
8c										X	X		
9a									X				X
9b								X					
9c								X					

91

PREACHING	TEACHING	KNOWLEDGE	WISDOM	EXHORTATION	FAITH	DISCERNMENT OF SPIRITS	HELPS	SERVING	ADMINISTRATION	RULING	MERCY	GIVING	
												X	9c
X								X	X	X			10a
							X				X		10b
								X					11a
								X	X	X			11b
							X	X			X	X	11c
									X				12a
									X	X			12b
						X							12c
									X		X		13a
							X						13b
			X										13c
		X											14a
				X	X			X			X	X	14b
			X			X			X	X			14c
											X		15a
							X						15b
												X	16a
												X	16b
									X	X		X	16c
					X								16d
												X	16e
							X	X	X	X		X	17a
	X	X	X										17b
				X							X		17c
X					X	X							17d
X													18a
	X												18b
		X											18c
		X											18d
TOTAL CIRCLED													
% CIRCLED													

	Total Circled	%	Total Circled	%
PERCENTAGES	1	10	6	60
	2	20	7	70
	3	30	8	80
	4	40	9	90
	5	50	10	100

	PREACHING	TEACHING	KNOWLEDGE	WISDOM	EXHORTATION	FAITH	DISCERNMENT OF SPIRITS	HELPS	SERVING	ADMINISTRATION	RULING	MERCY	GIVING
a	X	X									X		
b		X	X	X	X	X	X			X			
c												X	
a	X	X			X								
b		X	X		X	X	X			X			
c					X			X				X	
a					X			X	X			X	X
b	X	X			X						X	X	
c			X										
d				X	X		X						
a	X												
b		X											
c			X										
d				X									
e					X								
a				X	X							X	
b	X	X	X										
c	X				X			X	X	X			
a						X							
b						X							
c						X							
a						X							
b					X	X							
a	X	X	X										
b					X		X						
c											X	X	
a									X				X
b								X					
c								X					

PREACHING	TEACHING	KNOWLEDGE	WISDOM	EXHORTATION	FAITH	DISCERNMENT OF SPIRITS	HELPS	SERVING	ADMINISTRATION	RULING	MERCY	GIVING
												X
X								X	X	X		
							X				X	
							X					
							X	X	X			
							X	X			X	X
									X			
									X	X		
						X						
									X		X	
							X					
			X									
		X										
				X	X			X			X	X
		X			X				X	X		
											X	
					X							
												X
												X
									X	X		X
					X							
												X
							X	X	X	X		X
	X	X	X									
					X						X	
X					X	X						
X												
	X											
		X										
		X										
TOTAL CIRCLED												
% CIRCLED												

PERCENTAGES	Total Circled	%	Total Circled	%
	1	10	6	60
	2	20	7	70
	3	30	8	80
	4	40	9	90
	5	50	10	100

	PREACHING	TEACHING	KNOWLEDGE	WISDOM	EXHORTATION	FAITH	DISCERNMENT OF SPIRITS	HELPS	SERVING	ADMINISTRATION	RULING	MERCY	GIVING
1a	X	X									X		
1b		X	X	X	X	X	X			X			
1c												X	
2a	X	X			X								
2b		X	X	X		X	X			X			
2c				X				X				X	
3a					X			X	X			X	X
3b	X	X				X					X	X	
3c			X										
3d				X	X		X						
4a	X												
4b		X											
4c			X										
4d				X									
4e					X								
5a				X	X							X	
5b	X	X	X										
5c	X			X				X	X	X			
6a						X							
6b						X							
6c						X							
7a							X						
7b					X	X							
8a	X	X	X										
8b					X		X						
8c											X	X	
9a									X				X
9b								X					
9c								X					

95

PREACHING	TEACHING	KNOWLEDGE	WISDOM	EXHORTATION	FAITH	DISCERNMENT OF SPIRITS	HELPS	SERVING	ADMINISTRATION	RULING	MERCY	GIVING	
												X	9d
X								X	X	X			10a
							X				X		10b
								X					11a
								X	X	X			11b
							X	X			X	X	11c
									X				12a
									X	X			12b
						X							12c
									X		X		13a
							X						13b
			X										13c
		X											14a
				X	X			X			X	X	14b
			X		X				X	X			14c
											X		15a
							X						15b
												X	16a
												X	16b
									X	X		X	16c
				X									16d
												X	16e
							X	X	X	X		X	17a
	X	X	X										17b
				X							X		17c
X					X	X							17d
X													18a
	X												18b
		X											18c
		X											18d
TOTAL CIRCLED													
% CIRCLED													

PERCENTAGES

Total Circled	%	Total Circled	%
1	10	6	60
2	20	7	70
3	30	8	80
4	40	9	90
5	50	10	100

NINE
Evaluation Four:
Past Christian Service Experiences

Instructions:

A. List below the areas of church ministry in which you have served in the past; evaluate them according to the categories given. Place a check mark on the line below high, average, or low evaluation for each area of service and for each method of evaluation.

Areas of service	Degree of motivation to do the task			Sense of personal accomplishment			Fruits which resulted		
	high	*avg.*	*low*	*high*	*avg.*	*low*	*high*	*avg.*	*low*
___	___	___	___	___	___	___	___	___	___
___	___	___	___	___	___	___	___	___	___
___	___	___	___	___	___	___	___	___	___
___	___	___	___	___	___	___	___	___	___
___	___	___	___	___	___	___	___	___	___
___	___	___	___	___	___	___	___	___	___
___	___	___	___	___	___	___	___	___	___

B. In connection with the above evaluations, were there any special circumstances which affected your response that would not be true of a normal situation? If so, explain.

_____

_____

_____

C. Your feelings and concerns about your church and other churches will often be an indicator of your gifts. With that in mind, respond below to the following questions:

1. What kinds of needs in your church do you strongly believe must be met? (i.e. educational, financial, personal, social, etc.) _____

_____

2. Does your concern for these needs give you any insights into what your gifts may be? If so, list those gifts and explain why you think there is a connection between your concern and the gifts. ____

_____
_____
_____

3. Where would you most like to serve if the
   opportunities were available and you were trained?
   _____
   _____

4. Does your desire in question 3 give you any
   insights into what your gifts may be? If so, write
   down what those gifts are and why you think there
   is a connection between your interest and the gifts.
   _____
   _____
   _____
   _____

D. Based upon the assessments in evaluations *A* and *B*
above, and upon your understanding of the spiritual gifts
already studied, turn to the next section.

Holly – 70%
Admin – 60%
Giving
wisdom
Helps

SUMMARY OF PERSONAL EVALUATIONS

1. Based on my assessment of my preferences using the
   multiple choice indicator, I appear to have one of the
   following gifts:

   a. Mercy – 56%   Mom for me   Megan
   b. Helps   Helps 90%   Faith – 60%
   c. Serving   Mercy   teaching
   d. Administration 50% serving 80%   Helps
   e. Giving   giving   Administration 50%

2. Based on others' assessment of my preferences, I appear
   to have one of the following gifts:

   a. Helps _____
   b. Giving _____
   c. Administration _____
   d. Mercy _____
   e. serving _____

3. Based on my evaluation of past Christian experiences, I
   appear to have which of the following gifts listed in
   either 1 or 2 above?

   a. _____
   b. _____
   c. _____
   d. _____
   e. _____

TEN
Evaluating Yourself against Each Gift

Through the foregoing study of spiritual gifts and the several evaluations of your own preferences and tendencies, you now have a basis upon which to make a final evaluation of your possible gift(s). As you think through the following summaries of the thirteen spiritual gifts, look for the one or more most closely aligned with your evaluations. Be praying that God will give you true wisdom in this judgment.

Instructions:
  A. Using the evaluations of your preferences and past experiences, analyze the following definitions of the gifts with a view to determining which one(s) you might have.
  B. Under the evaluation section for each gift, complete the sentence by underlining either *(may)* or *(may not)*, and by giving the reason for your conclusion.
  C. Summarize your conclusions at the end of this chapter.

Descriptions of each gift

I. SPEAKING GIFTS
  A. Prophecy—the God-given ability to take the truth of God in the Bible and speak it forth with the result that lives are changed (see Romans 12:6).
    Tendencies of a person with this gift:
    1. Prefers speaking to groups over individual interaction
    2. Carefully studies Scripture before speaking
    3. Exhorts, teaches, and consoles in his/her messages, rather than doing just one of these three.
    4. Urges others to make big decisions immediately, rather than working for long-range, small changes in behavior
    5. May have difficulty in being sensitive to and patient with individuals' problems
    Evaluation: I *(may)* *(may not)* have this gift because

  B. Teaching—the God-given ability to systematically and

effectively organize and explain the principles of the Bible (see Romans 12:7).
Tendencies of a person with this gift:
1. Relies definitely and assuredly on the authority of the Scriptures
2. Delights in research and systematic presentation of truth
3. Is tenacious about keeping verses in context and being accurate in every statement made
4. Prefers a public ministry (for which he/she can prepare) to individual counseling
5. Tends to be critical of others with different positions on biblical doctrine
6. Has a balanced emphasis on logic, word meanings, and practical application for life changes
Evaluation: I *(may) (may not)* have this gift because

_____

_____

C. Word of knowledge—the God-given ability to translate and interpret biblical truth for preaching and teaching (see 1 Corinthians 12:8).
Tendencies of a person with this gift:
1. Has interest in and places emphasis on the doctrines of Scripture, i.e., nature of God, God's eternal plans, etc., and mentally grasps the way these pieces of knowledge fit into the whole of doctrine.
2. Shows ability to understand and remember doctrine; may tend to measure the degree of spiritual maturity in others mainly by the amount of biblical knowledge they retain
3. Emphasizes knowledge in a passage more than its life-relatedness
4. Finds practical applications of Scripture and counseling to be difficult tasks
Evaluation: I *(may) (may not)* have this gift because

_____

_____

D. Word of wisdom—the God-given ability to take the knowledge of God's Word and apply it by principles and insights to practical living (see 1 Corinthians 12:8).

Tendencies of a person with this gift:
1. Has interest in biblical truth as it applies to conduct
2. Emphasizes the more practical portions of Scripture for study
3. Places careful emphasis on attaining insight regarding the Lord's will
4. Has no intense interest in (and may question the value of) in-depth doctrinal studies
5. Is suspicious of all nonbiblical insights from life and the social sciences, because of unique appreciation for the scriptural perspective
6. Will tend more toward unifying people than causing division based on doctrinal differences

Evaluation: I *(may) (may not)* have this gift because

_____

_____

E. Exhortation—the God-given ability to come alongside others to encourage, counsel, and console them, using the Scriptures (see Romans 12:8).

Tendencies of a person with this gift:
1. Identifies emotionally and mentally with others in their predicaments
2. Visualizes goals and steps of action for others to follow
3. Appeals to the will by asking, urging, and requesting certain courses of action publicly
4. Speaks with a sense of urgency, appearing at times to oversimplify problems because of confidence in steps of action prescribed
5. May have personal struggles with studying the Scriptures in depth because of greater concern for practical applications from surface reading
6. May use the Scriptures more to support or illustrate his/her practical insight, than as the base from which true interpretation and application come

Evaluation: I *(may) (may not)* have this gift because

_____

_____

II. SERVING GIFTS
A. Faith—the God-given ability to exercise

wonder-working faith, to see beyond the problems and needs to the resource, God (see 1 Corinthians 12:9).
Tendencies of a person with this gift:
1. Has a strong belief in and reliance on God when foresight and future goals are involved
2. Desires to see seemingly impossible tasks accomplished
3. Provides continual vision for others amid seemingly hopeless situations
4. Has feelings of impatience with logical, cautious thinkers
5. Is concerned with end goals and tends to overlook details, considering them unimportant
6. Is usually not responsive to counsel and refinements of his/her goals
Evaluation: I *(may)* *(may not)* have this gift because

_____

_____

B. Discernment of spirits—the God-given ability to differentiate between the sources of man's speech and actions, whether from the Holy Spirit or from some other spirit (see 1 Corinthians 12:10).
Tendencies of a person with this gift:
1. Gives in to his impulse to probe people in order to ascertain their true spiritual character
2. Is quick to analyze the reasonings and rationalizations of others
3. Has profound sense of right and wrong
4. Assists others in identifying root spiritual problems
5. Has a tendency to render judgments on people's spiritual condition, and thus avoids helping them to see the needed process of change
Evaluation: I *(may)* *(may not)* have this gift because

_____

_____

C. Helps—the God-given ability to be willing and available to help out in any area in which there is a need (see 1 Corinthians 12:28).
Tendencies of a person with this gift:
1. Is deeply impressed with biblical exhortations to serve other Christians
2. Is sensitive to meeting the immediate needs of

people when called upon or when any need(s) come
to his/her attention
3. Does not seek a leadership position, but seeks to
serve under someone else
4. Prefers to respond to a need which does not require
preparation time and organizational detail
5. Does not emphasize finishing tasks or verbally
witnessing for Christ
Evaluation: I *(may) (may not)* have this gift because

_____

_____

D. Serving—the God-given ability to meet the needs,
   especially the material needs, of others (see Romans
   12:7).
   Tendencies of a person with this gift:
   1. Is self-motivated to serve others and meet their
      immediate needs without others' leadership;
      frustrated by long-range goals of any kind
   2. Visualizes fulfillment of practical needs of people as
      opposed to deeper spiritual needs
   3. Has a tendency to overinvolvement because of
      sensitivity to practical needs of people in the
      church; personal priorities may suffer
   4. Desires tasks to be done with high quality and
      enthusiasm
   5. May appear pushy and irritated by policies and red
      tape, due to desire to get things done
   Evaluation: I *(may) (may not)* have this gift because

_____

_____

E. Administration—the God-given ability to guide and
   direct the workings of the church with skill (see
   1 Corinthians 12:4).
   Tendencies of a person with this gift:
   1. Aspires to positions which require charting courses
      of action and decision making
   2. Is conscious of efficiency and order (or lack of
      order) within the church
   3. Can carry on discussions, summarize, draw
      conclusions, and often harmonize the best from
      various points of view
   4. Has a tendency to be so convinced of his/her own

opinions that he/she stifles discussion and resents
opposition
Evaluation: I *(may)* *(may not)* have this gift because

F. Ruling—the God-given ability to stand before others
to preside and effectively lead others with care and
diligence (see Romans 12:8).
Tendencies of a person with this gift:
1. Has a compulsion for church business to be done in
an orderly fashion, and inwardly reacts with strong
feelings toward inadequate procedures
2. Has ability and interest in learning to lead
3. Is more naturally concerned with overall
organizational objectives and programs than with
the feelings and individual spiritual needs of others
4. May desire and actually carry out a thorough job of
· leading Bible studies
5. Tends to assume leadership, organize, and delegate
responsibilities if no assigned leader exists in a
group
Evaluation: I *(may)* *(may not)* have this gift because

G. Mercy—the God-given ability to show compassion for
the misery of others and to relieve the problem with a
true attitude of cheerfulness (see Romans 12:8).
Tendencies of a person with this gift:
1. Is cheerful, noncondemning, compassionate, and
sensitive to others' distresses
2. Is quick to respond to others' needs for help
3. Attracts those with inward struggles because he/she
is sympathetic, conveying an air of understanding
4. Lacks firmness and decisiveness since he/she is so
sensitive toward possibly offending others
5. Resents others who are not as sensitive as he/she is
to personal needs
Evaluation: I *(may)* *(may not)* have this gift because

H. Giving—the God-given ability to give liberally with
love and joy (see Romans 12:8).

Tendencies of a person with this gift:
1. Is sensitive to the material needs of others and desires to meet those needs without publicity
2. Is always ready to give; can make quick decisions regarding helping others in their needs
3. Has the ability to gain wealth and make wise investments
4. Works hard in order to have enough to share with others; keeps that goal in his/her mind rather than only adding to personal wealth
5. May measure the spiritual maturity of others by the percentage of income or the absolute amount they give to the church and Christian organizations

Evaluation: I *(may)* *(may not)* have this gift because

_____

_____

CONCLUSION. As a result of this evaluation and in conjunction with the other evaluations, I believe I may have one of the following spiritual gifts:

1. _____

2. _____

3. _____

4. _____

5. _____

ELEVEN
Making
a Commitment

Now that you have determined the possible areas of your spiritual gift, you can test whether or not you have a given gift by serving. The following partial list of church ministry opportunities is classified according to spiritual gifts. The abilities necessary to accomplish these tasks are often found in those with the spiritual gift listed. Prayerfully determine the top three or four gifts you want to test; then, go through the list of ministries under each of the gifts you are interested in testing. Check those you would consider tackling.

Preaching

boards and commissions
  elder
  deacon
  evangelism

Bible teacher
  migrant worker
  prisons
  hospitals
  rest homes

military

pastor

missionary
  church planting
  evangelism

gospel teams
  evangelistic services
  speaker

Teaching

boards and commissions
  elder
  deacon
  Christian education

church services
  toddler church
  beginner church
  primary church

home visitation

young people
  Pioneer Girls
  King's Sons
  Christian Service
    Brigade

Boy Scouts
Girl Scouts

outreach
  gospel team
  small group home Bible
    study leader

Sunday school
  superintendent
  assistant superintendent
  department coordinator
  children's teacher
  youth teacher
  adult teacher
  substitute teacher

vacation Bible school
  committee
  teacher
  assistant

missionary-teacher

international student
  ministry
    teacher

Knowledge

boards and commissions
  elder
  deacon
  Christian education

young people
  Pioneer Girls
  King's Sons
  Christian Service
    Brigade
  Boy Scouts
  Girl Scouts

outreach
  small group home Bible
    study discussion leader

Sunday school
  superintendent
  assistant superintendent
  youth teacher
  adult teacher

vacation Bible school
  teacher

missionary
  translation
  interpretation—com-
    mentaries

research
  Sunday school
    curriculum
  Bible school curriculum

Wisdom

boards and commissions
  elder
  deacon
  trustee
  school commission
  building commission
  finance commission

librarian

outreach
  home visitation
  small group home Bible
    study leader
  gospel teams

young people

youth sponsors
  Pioneer Girls
  King's Sons
  Christian Service
    Brigade
  Boy Scouts
  Girl Scouts
  teen week speaker

counseling
  vocational
  minority group
    programs
  gang ministries
  marriage
  homosexuals

divorced
released prisoners
widows and widowers

missionary
  planning

church planting
school instruction

vacation Bible school
  director

Exhortation

boards and commissions
  elder
  deacon
  Christian education

Church services
  toddler
  beginner
  primary
  adult
  vocal music
  usher
  greeter

visitation
  sick
  newcomers
  shut-ins
  canvassing
  members
  prison
  hospital
  rest homes
  telephone

young people
  Pioneer Girls
  King's Sons

Christian Service
  Brigade
  Boy Scouts
  Girl Scouts

outreach
  gospel teams

counselor
  emotionally disturbed
  divorced
  premarital
  gangs
  homosexuals
  juvenile offenders
  marriage conflicts
  narcotic addicts
  potential suicides
  released prison
    offenders
  runaway youths
  school dropouts
  widows and widowers
  camp

vacation Bible school
  teacher

Faith

boards and commissions
  elder
  deacon
  trustee

nominating committee
missionary commission
building commission
school commission

outreach
  home visitation
  gospel teams
  evangelism

missionary
  church planting

Discernment of Spirits

boards and commissions
  elder
  deacon
  membership commission
  Christian education
    commission
  nominating committee
  missionary commission
  school commission

personnel recruitment

outreach
  home visitation

young people
  youth sponsors

counselor
  church
  camp
  juvenile offenders
  marriage conflicts
  divorced
  neglected children
  neglectful parents
  runaway youth
  potential suicide
  school dropouts

librarian
Sunday school
  adult

Helps

boards and commissions
  deaconess
  social commission
  trustee
  finance commission
  property commission
  school commission
  building commission

officers
  treasurer
  financial secretary
  clerk

church services
  usher
  greeter

librarian

nursery
  coordinator
  assistant

missionary
  women's missionary
    circle leader
  White Cross worker

men's fellowship
  committee

outreach
  gospel teams-trans-
    portation
  Bible school host/hostess
  Home Bible study
    host/hostess

Sunday school
  secretary
  departmental secretary

music
  chancel choir director
  youth choir director
  children's choir director
  song leader
  choir member
  soloist
  trio
  quartet
  duet
  pianist—accompanist
         —soloist
  organist
  instrumentalist
  orchestra leader
  music committee

bus driver

banquet worker

office help
  type
  draw
  file
  assemble
  reproduce materials
  mailings
  telephoning
  record information
  key punching

hospitality
  meals
  lodging

transportation
  shut-ins
  youth activities
  church services

bus driver—conventional
         —diesel

cook

nurse

kitchen help

athletic teams
  basketball
  baseball/softball
  volleyball
  swimming
  football
  other _____

maintenance
  landscaping
  carpentry
  painting
  electrical
  plumbing
  cleaning

artistic work

financial
  accounting
  bookkeeping
  money counting
  computer

audiovisual
  video-taping
  projectionist
  filing
  printer/posters
  television
  photographer
  artist
  tape recorder

Sunday school
  hear memory work
  secretary

helper
 deaf
 blind
 narcotic addicts
 alcoholics
 mentally ill
 migrant workers
 remedial reading
 nursing

underprivileged
 mentally retarded

library bookbinding

radio booth
 sound engineer

drama—acting

Serving

officers
 financial secretary
 treasurer

librarian

greeter

building committee

nursery coordinator

young people
 Pioneer Girls
 King's Sons
 Christian Service
  Brigade
 Boy Scouts
 Girl Scouts

women's missionary
 circles

men's fellowship

music
 song leader
 soloist
 instrumentalist

nurse

kitchen help

handyman

carpenter

church drama productions

financial

accounting

audiovisual
 video-taping
 projectionist
 television
 photographer

helper
 narcotic addicts
 alcoholics
 migrant workers
 nursing
 underprivileged

music
 chancel choir director
 youth choir director
 children's choir director
 song leader
 choir member
 soloist
 trio
 duet
 quartet
 pianist—accompanist
       —soloist
 organist
 instrumentalist
 orchestra leader

music committee

office help
  type
  telephone

hospitality
  meals
  lodging

Administration

boards and commissions
  deacon
  trustee
  deaconess
  Christian education
  missionary
  school
  property
  finance
  membership
  evangelistic
  church services
  social
  building
  planning

officers
  financial secretary
  treasurer
  head usher

nursery coordinator

young people
  youth sponsor
  youth committee
  single adults sponsor
  Pioneer Girls
  King's Sons
  Christian Service
    Brigade

women's missionary circle
  leader

men's fellowship leader

Sunday school
  assistant superintendent
  department
    coordinator—all
    ages
  class officer
  class committees

librarian
  cataloging

international student
  ministry

camp
  director
  assistant director
  administrative staff

radio booth operator

audiovisual room
  coordinator

drama directing

coffeehouse ministry

vacation Bible school
  director
  committee
  assistant

teen week director

Ruling

boards and commissions
  school board
  deacon
  trustee
  property
  finance
  building
  planning

church services
  greeter
  head usher

church moderator
  vice moderator

vacation Bible school
  director

teen week director

Sunday school
  superintendent
  department coordinator

men's fellowship leader

women's fellowship leader

women's missionary circle
  leader

camp director

class officers

Mercy

boards and commissions
  deacon
  deaconess

church services
  usher
  greeter

cassette ministry to
  shut-ins

hospitality
  meals
  lodging

visitation
  sick
  dying
  shut-ins
  hospitals
  rest homes
  telephone
  newcomers
  bereaved

missions
  committee
  missionary circles
  local gospel mission
  White Cross
  correspondent with
    missionaries
  furlough assistant

helper
  alcoholics
  mentally ill
  remedial reading
  nursing
  blind
  deaf
  gangs
  hungry and
    underprivileged
  mentally retarded
  migrant workers
  narcotic addict
  released prison
    offenders

boards and commissions
    trustee
    missionary commission
    fund raising commission
    building commission
    school commission
    planning and
        development
        commission
	food and money to help
	    poor
	
	hospitality
	    meals
	    lodging
	
	sponsor and underwrite
	    special missionary projects

FITTING INTO A PLACE OF SERVICE. Now that you have checked areas of service you are willing to try, it is time to make an appointment with your pastor, minister of Christian education, or other church worker who can assist you in finding a specific place to serve in your church.

If you have never served before, or have not served in the areas that are currently open, be sure to ask the church worker for training. Don't try to be so brave as to work without help until you have some training and experience.

After you have mutually agreed upon an area of service, and have arranged for proper training and supervision, fill out the "My Commitment" form that follows this page. Be prepared to really commit yourself to doing an excellent job. Excellence breeds confidence if you are serving in the area for which you are gifted. Without the commitment, you may miss the opportunity to affirm your gift, because you would not have worked hard enough to have a good experience. Determining your gift will take work, but will lead to many years of effective, satisfying, and fruitful service once you find it.

Upon completion of your commitment form, you will soon begin to be trained and to serve. After three months of experience, you will want to evaluate your progress on the "Gift Evaluation" form following the "commitment" form. In addition, your supervisor, or the one who is working the closest with you, will evaluate you on the "Supervisor Evaluation" form included in this chapter. This time of evaluation will be very helpful to you in determining whether or not you should continue to test the gift in the area of service to which you have committed yourself.

If it is mutually agreed that you should pursue another gift or area of service, contact your church worker in charge of placement, and repeat the process, beginning with paragraph one of this chapter. This process should be continued until you find a satisfying, challenging, and fruitful place of service in keeping with your spiritual gift. Having diligently studied and prayed as you worked through this manual, you will find that your gift will become evident before too long, if not in your first area of service.

MY COMMITMENT. After reviewing the various areas of service corresponding to the spiritual gifts, I am willing to serve the Lord in the following way as soon as a position can be obtained:

_____

   This service will help me determine if I have the spiritual gift of _____

   I will be trained and supervised in the following manner:

_____

_____

   I will be responsible for evaluating my progress (using the other forms provided) with one of the pastors or other spiritual leaders in the church. I will turn in these forms to the pastor by _____.
                            (date)
                    Signed _____
                    Date _____

GIFT EVALUATION FORM. Date of evaluation _____

Area of service completed _____

Spiritual gift tested _____

Describe the aspects of the work which you enjoyed most.

_____

_____

Describe the aspects of the work which you didn't enjoy. ___

_____

_____

What fruit did you see in your own life through your
service?_____

_____

_____

What fruit did you see in the lives of those you served? ___

_____

_____

Do you believe that more learning and experience could
possibly confirm the existence of this gift in you? _____

_____

Signed _____

Date _____

SUPERVISOR EVALUATION FORM. Name of worker ___

Date of evaluation _____
Area of service completed _____
Spiritual gift tested _____

Evaluate the above-named worker in the following areas.

1. Degree of spiritual motivation to do the task: _____
   _____
   _____

2. Degree of responsibility to the task: _____
   _____
   _____

3. Response of persons being served: _____
   _____
   _____

4. Do you believe he or she may have the
   above-mentioned spiritual gift? Explain. _____
   _____
   _____
   _____

                    Signed _____
                    Date _____

TWELVE
Mobilizing Your Church through Spiritual Gifts

Every church has a philosophy of ministry. A few churches have carefully developed and clearly understood the underlying principles that guide their ministries. In contrast, many churches have a rather haphazard philosophy that has emerged from a series of isolated program decisions by various leaders over the years. Out of these decisions, traditions have developed which determine the direction and kind of ministry the church now has.

Regardless of what has been accomplished in a church, one thing is clear: *A church must have a definite, biblically based statement of philosophy regarding its approach to involving people in service.* Until some key biblical principles for developing, training, and involving people are agreed upon and followed, a church will not serve one another at a top level of effectiveness.

The reason why a clear biblical philosophy of service is important is because it directly affects the climate in the church and the attitudes of the potential servers. Largely, the philosophy determines whether a church will be an organization or an organism.

In many churches, a prevailing principle regarding service is that the pastor(s) is (are) hired to do the work of the ministry and the members are to serve as assistants when invited. As a result, statements like "I'm going to church to listen to the pastor, for I like sitting under his ministry" are often made. Underlying this philosophy is the idea that God communicates to the pastor(s) what needs to be communicated to and accomplished by the church. The pastor(s) either handles the task himself (themselves) and/or invites (invite) others to share the load.

Until asked to serve, members have no particular responsibility but to attend and participate in the church activities of their choice. When they are asked to serve, they do a job until it is complete or until they want to be relieved. This type of church is a clear example of an organization, which is defined as a body of people where there are interdependent parts, each having a particular function normally assigned by the leadership.

The previously described kind of church climate is antithetical to the early church model given in the New Testament. At that time, there were very few full-time ministers. The philosophy was that the Body of Christ, the Church, was an organism, made up of all the members. As an organism, the individual parts had separate functions, but all were mutually dependent on the functioning of the rest for their survival. Each part served according to its designed function. When this happened, the needs of all the other parts were met and the organism grew and remained healthy.

A philosophy of service which will meet the biblical guidelines and maintain a church as a living organism must be founded on the principle that all the members are gifted to be contributors to the local church to which God has led them. Note 1 Corinthians 12:18, 25: "But now God has placed the members, each one of them, in the body, just as He desired . . . that the members should have the same care for one another" (NASB). *Everyone is responsible for the ministry.*

How is the climate created so that everyone believes and feels he is an essential contributor? First, the appropriate portions of the Word of God on spiritual gifts must be taught with emphasis on the giftedness and importance of every member to the church. Second, the leaders must be willing to share their gifts and give priority time to ministering primarily in their particular areas of strength. When the church benefits from the leaders' strengths, the members will want to encourage them to keep using their gifts. The people will, likewise be more willing to use their gifts to meet needs which the leaders aren't gifted to meet.

Third, the leaders must draw gifted people into service and indicate clearly to them that they are not assisting the leaders or doing them a favor by serving. It should be made clear that God has gifted them for service and placed them in the church specifically for a contribution to the whole. In addition, the leaders should offer classes, seminars, study groups, and so on for the dual purpose of studying the Scripture in detail about gifts and helping people determine their gifts. At the close of the study, participants should be given specific opportunities to become involved in serving if they are not currently active in areas related to their gifts.

A study which closes by leaving the participants with the general exhortation to "go now and get involved" has failed to create the right climate for the involvement of every member. Many people need specific counsel and encouragement to become involved. Further, class members should be asked to indicate on paper what they feel their gifts might be. They should be told that the leaders will file this information away for future use so that when opportunities arise in which their gifts might be used, they will be contacted. Then, rather than enlisting volunteers from the pulpit or bulletin, the leaders use their files. This process builds faith in the leaders' expressed intention of using gifted people in the ministry.

Next, the leaders need to foster a climate of appreciation for the contributions of all the members. The pastors, musicians, Sunday school teachers, and a few others are often the ones who receive recognition for their service. Ushers, class secretaries, custodians, committee members, nursery attendants, and so forth are easily overlooked. Member-appreciation night when people express thankfulness to God for others is one way to help develop an awareness of everyone's importance. Encouragement cards are also helpful. These postcard-sized response cards can be printed up and used by members to write out expressions of appreciation for the gifts and ministries of others. Keeping the pew racks or display tables stocked with these cards communicates to the people that it is important to church life to share thoughts of thankfulness.

Finally, some part of the church service should be given over to spontaneous member ministry through verbal sharing, musical messages, and other expressions. First Corinthians 14:26 says, ". . . what is the outcome then, brethren? When you assemble, each one has a psalm, has a teaching, has a revelation . . ." (NASB). While the Scripture clearly teaches orderliness in the church (1 Corinthians 14:40), this does not have to mean that every minute of every service is controlled and planned so tightly that spontaneous member ministry is impossible.

In summary, the environment in which people worship, receive education and training, and carry out their service is vital to determining how they think about themselves and their part in the church life and ministry. They will feel one of two things: they are part of an organization, bound by regulations, policies, fixed programs, and traditions, or they are a part of a living organism, and can move among its members in informal and formal settings, serving and being served, feeling invaluable to the health and development of the entire body. The latter attitude and feeling must be taught and caught by most of the membership if a church is to be alive and well.

WHO DECIDES WHAT THE CHURCH WILL DO? In publicly held corporations, the stockholders have the right to recommend direction and policies to the management of the company. Usually, the management recommends that the stockholders vote against any recommendation by fellow stockholders. This kind of approach by management leaves the definite impression with the stockholders that their place is to invest money and approve management recommendations and that is all. It is not their place to suggest what the company should be involved in but to leave that to corporate management.

Church leaders can give a similar impression to the gifted members by the way they go about leading. In fact, unless a definite attempt is made to encourage member involvement in the direction of the church, the members will assume they are not to recommend changes and ideas unless specifically requested to do so.

The analogy of the church as a body indicates something significant about how the church body develops and remains healthy. In the human body, the head gives direction to various parts based on what needs to be accomplished to maintain health, reach goals, and so on. In the church body, Jesus Christ is the Head (Ephesians 1:22, 4:15, 5:23). We would assume that Christ as the head would communicate to the various members what needs to be accomplished according to each one's giftedness and would stimulate ministries also in accordance with each one's giftedness. If all the gifted members perfectly discerned the exact desire of God for the church of which they were members, their actions would always be appropriate to the needs of the body and thus build it up.

The need for spiritual leadership in the body arises simply because members are at various stages of spiritual maturity and do not always generate mature, wise ideas and ministries. Many churches overreact to the potential weaknesses of the members' ideas and do not encourage them to develop ministries at all. This is unfortunate. As is always the case with a balanced approach, members should be encouraged to take the responsibility of watching out for needs in the body that are being unmet and be thinking, out of their own gifted perspective, how those needs can be met. The leadership should respond with openness to any suggestions and take seriously what is being communicated. With maturity and wisdom, leaders should refine the suggestions and give thought to the timing and implementation of suggested ministries. Usually an attempt should be made to involve the person who initiated the suggestion. Because the person has his heart in it—because he senses God's leading—he is a natural for igniting the interest and involvement of others. Most church leaders agree that the hardest quality to find when looking for leaders for particular ministries is the deeply felt heart-desire to see particular ministries succeed. When a person has a God-given vision for something, then training, implementation, follow-through, and enthusiasm follow much more readily.

The leadership must not be threatened by the creativity and ministry vision of the members. Once it is understood that the Holy Spirit speaks on behalf of Christ to individual members in stimulating them to be involved in various ministries, there need be no fear; after all, in such a leading, Christ is functioning as the Head of his local church.

While a church is working at establishing the right climate and encouraging members to become involved in the process of ministry formulation, specific instruction and follow-up concerning spiritual gifts should be taking place. Classes on gift discovery should be offered on a regular yearly basis, preferably during the Sunday school hour. For those who constantly serve during that hour, an additional class should be offered at another time convenient to their schedules. As the class is being completed, one person or a team of people who are familiar with how gifts are and can be used in the church should be invited to the class to present the current needs and encourage participants in ways they may become involved.

Some churches have added a full-time staff person in gift discovery and ministry placement.

A spiritual gifts file system should be set up to store information on the members' gifts. This gives the church leadership almost instant access to the names of gifted people and helps them fill ministry vacancies as well as open new areas of ministry with greater ease. No business ever hires the first volunteer without regard for his qualifications for the job. Likewise, appeals for church volunteers should be kept to a minimum so that gifted people will not end up ministering in areas in which they are not gifted.

Ideally, this process results in a group of gifted members taking their appropriate places in the body under the direction of the Holy Spirit and the guidance of the local church leaders—a church mobilized for maximum ministry!

APPENDIXES

Appendix I
Planning a spiritual gifts seminar

II
Structuring a spiritual gifts seminar

III
Illustrated score sheet for evaluations
one and three

IV
Guide to interpreting the results of
evaluation one

V
Guide to interpreting the results of
evaluation three

APPENDIX I
Planning a
Spiritual Gifts Seminar

Leader preparation

This manual has been designed to give you an adequate background of information necessary to hold a spiritual gifts seminar. A thorough understanding of the biblical material and the evaluations is necessary. You should be able to clearly distinguish between the spiritual gifts after studying the sections called "Understanding the gifts" and "Evaluating yourself against each gift." The evaluation instructions and scoring can be mastered by doing the evaluations on yourself.

The following sections in this appendix will outline various concerns which you should take note of in overall planning.

Advance notice of the seminar

Promotion of the seminar should begin two months before the first session. The kind of publicity needed will depend on how much the people know about the subject of spiritual gifts. Some will be ready to sign up immediately after hearing of its nature and purpose. Others may be either unfamiliar with or confused by the subject and, therefore, not naturally responsive to general publicity. Both of these groups must become vitally interested through initial advertising.

Well-worded, descriptive announcements made during regular church services and in special bulletin inserts will build interest. These communications should contain stimulating appeals as to why every Christian should know and be using his spiritual gift. A key verse like 1 Peter 4:10, which shows that every Christian has a gift that he or she is to use, will help motivate them biblically. Testimonies from church members who are using their gifts will add a personal touch.

Three Sundays prior to the beginning of the seminar, all people (high school and above) who want to be involved should sign up. A posted list or bulletin insert with a registration section can be used. The time, place, cost, and duration of the course should be clearly shown. Posters and other spot reminders to register are helpful, also.

Encouraging those who are already serving

In every church there are faithful people who are serving Christ diligently. They may feel reasonably happy and fulfilled in their tasks. These people will be tempted to conclude that they do not need a seminar which stresses service. However, if they are not sure what their gifts are, they will lack a full, biblically based assurance that they are serving exactly where Christ would have them. When such people realize they have specific spiritual gifts to enable them to serve with power, their confidence and their effectiveness is greatly increased.

There are other benefits, too, for active Christians who know their spiritual gifts. First, they are saved from serving unsatisfyingly in positions that require spiritual gifts they do not possess. Too, they are rescued from taking on tasks inconsistent with the proper exercise of their gift.

Every participant in the church who does not know for certain what his gift is should take the seminar. For the uninvolved, it will provide the first step toward serving, and for those who are already serving, it will lead to maximum fruitfulness and confidence.

The need for giving personal help

Some people will not be able to grasp the material in the manual and work through it successfully on their own. Others may become confused at one point or another in the study, and feel incapable of completing it. Therefore, the leaders must always be available to give personal help when needed. Assisting someone to understand the biblical teaching on gifts, to evaluate himself or herself spiritually, and to find his or her peculiar area of service, is one of the most profitable uses of time. (See Ephesians 4:12-16.)

Determining church needs

Each gifted Christian is led to a local church to contribute to that spiritual body. Each individual is essential and must have a place to serve. No church is given an excess of gifted people who are not needed.

Since a spiritual gifts seminar brings to the surface gifted people, a list of current, challenging ministries must be prepared so each person can begin serving promptly. If the seminar is offered each year, an updated list of church needs, plus the gifts to be exercised in filling each need, should be available at all times.

The list of needs should include current tasks which need to be done to keep the present ministries fully staffed. In addition, a list of creative tasks which the church isn't carrying out should be available. These creative jobs stimulate vision in the church and provide vital opportunities for those who are willing to serve in a new ministry.

The pastor, Christian education director, and/or church ministry coordinators (Sunday school department heads, Sunday school superintendent, vacation Bible school coordinators, head usher, music director, etc.) should meet together for an orientation period prior to the beginning of the seminar. Each leader should draw up a list of service needs in his area by the fifth week of the seminar. When completed, the lists should be given to the pastor or other person conducting the seminar. The seminar leader must then decide which spiritual gifts might be exercised in meeting each need. See an example of this analysis below.

Training those who have made commitments

The key to moving people from the seminar into effective service with their gifts is training. This might be done in a large group, a small group, or on an individual basis. The extent of need for training and the number of capable instructors in the church will determine what a church can do. Ultimately, the training will have to fit each church's situation. However, one thing is certain: the newly committed seminar graduates must be helped.

Example of church needs with suggested spiritual gifts:

CENTRAL BAPTIST CHURCH
PRESENT NEEDS ANALYZED BY SPIRITUAL GIFTS

Area of need	Coordinator	Gifts used to meet needs
SUNDAY SCHOOL		
beginner dept.		
adult helper	dept. head	exhortation, serving, helps

Area of need	Coordinator	Gifts used to meet needs
primary dept. record keeper	dept. head	helps, admin.
junior dept. pianist	dept. head	helps, serving
young single adult teacher	S. S. supt.	teaching, exhortation knowledge

WEDNESDAY NIGHT

Christian Service Brigade committee member	boy's work chairman	serving, admin., wisdom, discernment of spirits

MUSIC

children's choir director	music dir.	admin., helps, serving
soloist	music dir.	exhortation, helps, serving

OUTREACH

evangelistic calling	outreach director	wisdom, mercy, exhortation
home Bible study leader	H.B.S. leader	teaching, wisdom
gospel teams	outreach director	preaching, exhortation, faith

COMMITTEE MEMBERS

missionary	nominating committee	faith, admin., mercy, giving
property	nominating committee	wisdom, admin., helps, giving

APPENDIX II
Structuring a Spiritual Gifts Seminar

There is no single, inflexible way of taking a group of Christians through the study on spiritual gifts. The studies can be broken down into a number of parts and taken one at a time. The manual lends itself very well to a one-quarter Sunday school class. This usually leaves three or four weeks at the end for further exploring any particularly important aspect of the study, or for studying material on the miraculous spiritual gifts and office gifts which this manual does not cover.

The illustration presented below explains one way of developing the seminar. It demonstrates how to coordinate the materials and the students' efforts.

Each session is scheduled for one hour. Obviously, the amount of time will depend on the size and makeup of the group. The tasks to be completed for each week are included under that week's responsibilities.

First Week Session

LEADER'S RESPONSIBILITIES

1. Have a registration sheet ready to circulate which requests name, address, and phone number of the student.
2. Type an attendance sheet in alphabetical order and provide boxes for checking attendance each week.
3. Present a general introduction and survey of the manual's content. Emphasize the importance of the study to your own church or group.

STUDENT'S RESPONSIBILITIES

1. Purchase the manual and attend the session.
2. Commit yourself to faithfully following through each week by completing the assigned study.
3. Pray that God will give you spiritual wisdom and insight regarding your gift so that you might maximize your service for him.

LEADER'S RESPONSIBILITIES   STUDENT'S RESPONSIBILITIES

4. Ask for any questions concerning the course as a whole.
5. Assign the study in chapter one through the section on "Spiritual gifts."
6. Lead the group into the material in chapter one as time allows, helping them fill in some answers.

Second Week Session
1. Discuss the material assigned in chapter one, item by item. Have the students look up selected passages, but not all. Call on people from the roll so they won't come to class unprepared, thinking they can look up the answer at the time they are questioned.
2. Have each student tear out four copies of the assessment form two on page 73. These forms are to be filled in by the four available people who know the person best. Explain clearly how to complete the form. Tell the students they have six weeks to give out the forms, get them back, and compile the results. As the forms are returned, they should be scored.

1. Be prepared to discuss chapter one as assigned at the last session.

3. Assign the study in chapter two on the first seven gifts.

Third Week Session

1. Discuss the material assigned in chapter two on the first seven gifts.
2. Assign the study in chapter two on the last six gifts.
3. Direct interested students to use the Spiritual Gifts Inventory (SGI) in chapter seven and mail it to Dr. McMinn.

1. Be prepared to discuss the study on the first seven spiritual gifts.
2. Select the four people to whom you will give the evaluation forms, and give or mail them along with an explanation of instructions.

Fourth Week Session

1. Discuss the material assigned in chapter two on the last six spiritual gifts.
2. Assign the study of chapters three and four.

1. Be prepared to discuss the study on the last six gifts.
2. If using the SGI, be sure you fill it out completely and mail it to Dr. McMinn. See chapter seven for the address.

Fifth Week Session

1. Discuss the material assigned in chapters three and four.
2. Assign the study of chapter five through "Personal preparation before using the gifts."

1. Be prepared to discuss the study on chapters three and four.

Sixth Week Session

1. Discuss the material assigned in chapter five.
2. Assign the study of the remainder of chapter five.

1. Be prepared to discuss the material in chapter five that was assigned.
2. If you haven't received your evaluations back

LEADER'S RESPONSIBILITIES	STUDENT'S RESPONSIBILITIES

Seventh Week Session

1. Discuss the material assigned in the remainder of chapter five.
2. Assign the material in chapters six and nine.

Eighth Week Session

1. Discuss the evaluations.
   a. Resolve any questions students have in understanding the questionnaire.
   b. Show the students how to score the evaluations and have them complete the scoring in class.
   c. Explain how to fill in the summary on pages 98, 99 and have them complete it in class.
2. Assign the study of chapters ten and eleven.
3. Hand out a complete list of the present needs in your church (see sample copy on page 132). Encourage the students to make some tentative choices after completing the evaluation of each gift in chapter ten and checking the areas of interest in chapter eleven.
4. Encourage the students to pray that God will direct them to the place

(Student's column)

from others, contact them.

1. Be prepared to discuss the material for the remainder of chapter five.

1. Have the evaluation forms completed and be ready to score them.

137

where they should begin serving.

Ninth Week Session

1. Resolve any questions the students have in understanding the evaluation of themselves against each gift.
2. Have the ministry coordinators ready to talk with the students about service.
3. Explain the forms on pages 117, 119, 121.
4. Indicate to the group that you will be conducting a group evaluation session in about three months to assess overall progress of seminar participants.
5. Assign the study of chapter twelve. Encourage the group to think through the *meaning* and *implications* of the content of their reading for your own church situation. Be ready to discuss ways students can best help encourage mobilization within the church.

Tenth Week Session

1. Lead the discussion of chapter twelve.

1. Have the following complete:
   a. the evaluation of yourself against each gift.
   b. the selection of areas of service as given in chapter eleven that are consistent with your top four gift possibilities.
   c. the tentative selection of areas of service in your church which require your possible gifts.
2. Be prepared to sign a "My Commitment" form after consulting with one or more ministry coordinators who will be in attendance at the last session.

1. Be prepared to discuss the implications of chapter twelve for your church.

APPENDIX III
Illustrated Score Sheet for Evaluations One and Three

PERSONAL (AND OTHERS') ASSESSMENT
OF MY PREFERENCES AND TENDENCIES

1. I prefer situations in my church where I am:
   - ⓐ a speaker
   - b. in a discussion group
   - c. just a listener
2. If asked to speak, I prefer speaking to:
   - ⓐ large groups
   - ⓑ small groups
   - c. individuals

Score Sheet

	PREACHING	TEACHING	KNOWLEDGE	WISDOM	EXHORTATION	FAITH	DISCERNMENT OF SPIRITS	HELPS	SERVING	ADMINISTRATION	RULING	MERCY	GIVING	
	(X)	(X)									(X)			1a
		X	X	X	X	X	X			X				1b
												X		1c
	(X)	(X)			(X)									ⓐ
		(X)	(X)	(X)		(X)	(X)			(X)				ⓑ
									X		X			2c
														↓
							X							25h

	PREACHING	TEACHING	KNOWLEDGE	WISDOM	EXHORTATION	FAITH	DISCERNMENT OF SPIRITS	HELPS	SERVING	ADMINISTRATION	RULING	MERCY	GIVING
TOTAL CIRCLED	2	3	1	1	1	1	1	—	—	1	1	—	—
% CIRCLED	13	19	6	6	6	6	6	—	—	6	6	—	—

APPENDIX IV
Guide to Interpreting the Results of Evaluation One

After you finish Evaluation One, you may find that you have not yet been able to gain clear direction regarding your gift. The percentage of circled responses may be very similar for three or four gifts. You must now analyze the responses so as to determine your predominant preferences and tendencies.

In the multiple choice setting, you may have selected preferences that were true, given the options. However, if your selected preferences had been compared with one another, probably one of them would have been stronger than the others.

The following analysis describes each gift in terms of the preferences and tendencies of one with that gift. To use this analysis form, proceed in the following manner:

1. Note the names of the gifts for which you had the similar preference percentages.

    a._____

    b._____

    c._____

    d._____

    e._____

2. Take the score sheet and locate the column with the name of the gift noted in 1a above. Proceed down the column in search of the circled X's. Whenever you find a circled X, move across the score sheet from the X to the far left-hand column, where the numbered responses are given (2c, 3b, etc.).

3. After locating the numbered response corresponding to the circled X, proceed to the analysis of that gift below. Find the numbered response under the gift analysis which corresponds to the numbered response for the circled X in the score sheet. Circle that numbered response in the analysis.

4. Go back to the score sheet, find the second circled X and the corresponding numbered response, and circle that response under the same gift analysis below.

5. Repeat this procedure until all of the circled X's on the score sheet are also circled under the gift analysis below.

140

6. Repeat the procedure in 2 above for each of the gifts noted in 1.
7. Then analyze the results by the following inquiry:
   a. Compare the circled responses of all the gifts analyzed in 2 above, noting when a particular preference or tendency has been circled under more than one gift. For example, if preaching and teaching were two of the gifts being analyzed, under the analysis both would have circled preference 1a—"I prefer situations in which I am a speaker." Since there are a number of gifts which have the same preferences and tendencies, these should be noted.

Gifts with the same preferences	Preferences used twice or more
1)_____	_____
2)_____	_____
3)_____	_____
4)_____	_____
5)_____	_____
6)_____	_____
7)_____	_____

   b. Think over the remaining preferences which have not been circled twice, and try to discern if there seem to be three or four responses which are not exactly the same preference but could be considered similar. Summarize the similar preferences and tendencies below.

Gifts with similar preferences	Summary
1)_____	_____
2)_____	_____
3)_____	_____

   c. Taking the results in *a* and *b* above, decide which of the gifts in 1 above is most like these same and similar preferences. The decision may be difficult, but always remember that the evaluation is to be used only as a guide for purposes of channeling you into service. The ultimate determination of your gift will take place through service itself.
   d. The same and similar preferences and tendencies, along with overall analysis, seem to indicate that my gift might be_____

GIFT ANALYSIS
IN TERMS OF PREFERENCES AND TENDENCIES

I. Gift of Prophecy (Preaching)

1a I prefer situations in my church in which I am a speaker.

2a I prefer speaking to large groups.

3b When faced with counseling another person about his problems, I tend to give him the best biblical solution I can think of even if I'm not totally confident about my counsel.

4a When I begin to prepare for a talk to other Christians, I am normally motivated to emphasize the truths of basic Bible themes, so as to lead the listener to a clear-cut decision in the meeting.

6c When I approach my personal devotions, I most prefer to relate to the verses emotionally, so as to get a personal blessing.

7b If I have my choice of passages to study, I mostly choose ones which are very practical.

7d If I have my choice of passages to study, I mostly choose ones which have great emotional appeal to my Christian life.

8b When I give a testimony, I tend to indicate some area of doctrine that has come alive to me through an experience and/or verse I've shared.

8c When I give a testimony, I tend to emphasize the practical application of some verse(s) to my life.

11a When evaluating another Christian's spiritual condition, I tend to point out errors in his understanding of the Christian life.

13a In an organization, I prefer to lead a group.

20d If given a choice regarding involvement in a Sunday school class lesson, I tend to favor presenting the lesson with the content, illustrations, and applications available.

21a With regard to decisions made from my speaking, I prefer to see an immediate commitment at the meeting by individuals in the group.

23d When called upon to serve, I am most naturally

motivated to help in situations in which there are specific spiritual needs (for commitment, faith, dealing with sin, etc.).

24a When speaking before people, I sense an inner urgency to persuade people to make spiritual decisions and commitments right then.

24b When speaking before people I find it easy to accept the authority of the Scriptures without hesitation.

II. *Gift of Teaching*

1a I prefer situations in my church in which I am a speaker.

1b I prefer situations in my church in which I am in a discussion group.

2a I prefer speaking to large groups.

2b I prefer speaking to small groups.

3b When faced with counseling another person about his problems, I tend to give him the best biblical solution I can think of, even if I'm not totally confident about my counsel.

4b When I begin to prepare for a talk to other Christians, I am normally motivated to carefully organize a biblical passage in a systematic way, so that the listener clearly understands it.

5b When listening to others speak, I dislike talks which heavily emphasize illustrations and applications without logical order and doctrine.

6a When I approach my personal devotions, I most prefer to search out how the verses I'm studying add to my understanding of doctrine.

7a If I have my choice of passages to study, I mostly choose ones which are rich in doctrine.

7c If I have my choice of passages to study, I mostly choose ones which are controversial or difficult to understand.

8b When I give a testimony, I tend to indicate some area of doctrine that has come alive to me through an experience and/or verses I've shared.

11a When evaluating another Christian's spiritual condition, I tend to point out errors in his understanding of the Christian life.

20b If given a choice regarding involvement in a

Sunday school class lesson, I tend to favor organizing available content and illustrations for presentation of the truths.

21c With regard to decisions made from my speaking, I prefer to have an opportunity to explore the decision in depth through discussion.

23b When called upon to serve, I am most naturally motivated to help in situations in which there are specific mental needs (lack of understanding of Scripture, need to find God's will in a certain area, etc.).

24c When speaking before people, I am inwardly compelled to prepare well and speak carefully.

III. Gift of Knowledge

1b I prefer situations in my church in which I am in a discussion group.

2b I prefer speaking to small groups.

3c When faced with counseling another person about his problems, I tend to prefer sharing biblical insights, avoiding discussions about feelings.

4c When I begin to prepare for a talk to other Christians, I am normally motivated to instruct on doctrinal topics, to enable the listener to have a better understanding of these subject areas.

5b When listening to others speak, I tend to dislike talks which heavily emphasize illustrations and applications without logical order and doctrine.

6a When I approach my personal devotions, I most prefer to search out how the verses I'm studying add to my understanding of doctrine.

7a If I have my choice of passages to study, I mostly choose ones which are rich in doctrine.

7c If I have my choice of passages to study, I mostly choose ones which are controversial or difficult to understand.

8b When I give a testimony, I tend to indicate some area of doctrine that has come alive to me through an experience and/or verses I've shared.

11a When evaluating another Christian's spiritual condition, I tend to point out errors in his understanding of the Christian life.

17a My reaction to the needs of others tends to be slow because I don't know what to do.

20a If given a choice regarding involvement in a Sunday school class lesson, I would tend to favor doing the biblical research and study to provide the lesson content.

21c With regard to decisions made from my speaking, I prefer to have an opportunity to explore the decision in depth through discussion.

23b When called upon to serve, I am most naturally motivated to help in situations in which there are specific mental needs (lack of understanding Scripture, need to find God's will in a certain area, etc.).

24d When speaking before people, I have a tendency to encourage thought-life changes and decisions more than conduct changes.

24e When speaking before people, I feel most comfortable presenting a thorough, detailed study of a biblical passage or topic.

IV. *Gift of Wisdom*

1b I prefer situations in my church in which I am in a discussion group.

2b I prefer speaking to small groups.

2c I prefer speaking to individuals.

3d When faced with counseling another person about his problems, I tend to urge him to follow my counsel, because I honestly believe God often helps me to see solutions to others' problems.

4d When I begin to prepare for a talk to Christians, I am normally motivated to stress application of passages that emphasize practical truths so that the listener's conduct can be refined.

5a When listening to others speak, I tend to dislike in-depth doctrinal studies without applications.

6b When I approach my personal devotions, I most prefer to analyze the verses with the purpose of changing specific areas of my conduct.

7b If I have my choice of passages to study, I mostly choose ones which are very practical.

8c When I give a testimony, I tend to emphasize the practical application of some verse(s) to my life.

16d If a group is meeting and no assigned leader is there, I would tend to call someone to find out who the real leader is.

17c My reaction to the needs of others tends to be deliberate, because I want to make sure I've thought it through thoroughly.

20c If given a choice regarding involvement in a Sunday school class lesson, I would tend to favor thinking up original applications for the lesson, given the organized content.

21b With regard to decisions made from my speaking, I prefer to do follow-up counseling directed at long-range changes in conduct.

22b If I were a leader faced with two Christians in the church who couldn't get along, I would tend to talk to them about changing their attitudes.

23b When called upon to serve, I am most naturally motivated to help in situations in which there are specific mental needs (lack of understanding of Scripture, need to find God's will in a certain area, etc.)

24f When speaking before people, I have a tendency to give biblical insights on continually knowing and doing God's will.

V. Gift of Exhortation

1b I prefer situations in my church in which I am in a discussion group.

2a I prefer speaking to large groups.

3a When faced with counseling another person about his problems, I tend to identify deeply with his situation.

3d When faced with counseling another person about his problems, I tend to urge him to follow my counsel, because I honestly believe God often helps me see solutions to others' problems.

4e When I begin to prepare for a talk to other Christians, I am normally motivated to take one verse and outline practical, specific steps of action for the listener to follow.

5a When listening to others speak, I tend to dislike in-depth doctrinal studies without applications.

6b When I approach my personal devotions, I most

prefer to analyze the verses with the purpose of changing specific areas of conduct.

7b If I have my choice of passages to study, I mostly choose ones which are very practical.

8a When I give a testimony, I tend to encourage or console others rather than just share a verse or experience.

10b When conversing with other Christians, I tend to exhort them to embrace certain goals and actions.

11b When evaluating another Christian's spiritual condition, I tend to sense areas of right and wrong conduct in his life and point out some solutions.

17b My reaction to the needs of others tends to be quick because I usually sense what needs to be done.

21b With regard to decisions made from my speaking, I prefer to do follow-up counseling directed at long-range changes in conduct.

22b If I were a leader faced with two Christians in the church who couldn't get along, I would tend to talk to them about changing their attitudes.

23c When called upon to serve, I am most naturally motivated to help in situations in which there are specific emotional needs (fear, anxiety, frustration, moods due to pain or trials, etc.).

24g When speaking before people, I have a tendency to feel real concern for those in difficulty, and to suggest ways to help them.

VI. *Gift of Faith*
1b I prefer situations in my church in which I am in a discussion group.

2b I prefer speaking to small groups.

3b When faced with counseling another person about his problems, I tend to give him the best biblical solution I can think of, even if I'm not totally confident about my counsel.

6c When I approach my personal devotions, I most prefer to relate to the verses emotionally, so as to get a personal blessing.

7b If I have my choice of passages to study, I mostly choose ones which are very practical.

8a When I give a testimony, I tend to encourage or console others rather than just share a verse or experience.

9a With regard to planning for the future of my church, I tend to have confidence about what the church should do.

9c With regard to planning for the future of my church, I tend to be more concerned with envisioning end results than with the details involved in getting there.

9d With regard to planning for the future of my church, I tend to have a great desire to see quick growth in the church's ministries.

10b When conversing with other Christians, I tend to exhort them to embrace certain goals and actions.

15a If asked to lead in a church program somewhere, I would tend to choose a position which involved comprehensive planning for the future.

17b My reaction to the needs of others tends to be quick because I usually sense what needs to be done.

19e With regard to financial matters, I tend to see money as a means for carrying out ministries and meeting needs, more than for construction of buildings, payment of salaries, etc.

21a With regard to decisions made from my speaking, I prefer to see an immediate commitment at the meeting by individuals in the group.

23d When called upon to serve, I am most naturally motivated to help in situations in which there are specific spiritual needs (for commitment, faith, dealing with sin, etc.).

25a Generally speaking, I have a tendency to visualize future goals, and to work toward them in spite of difficulties.

VII. *Gift of Discernment of Spirits*

1b I prefer situations in my church where I am in a discussion group.

2b I prefer speaking to small groups.

3d When faced with counseling another person about his problems, I tend to urge him to follow my counsel, because I honestly believe God often helps me see solutions to others' problems.

6b When I approach my personal devotions, I most prefer to analyze the verses with the purpose of changing specific areas of my conduct.

7c If I have my choice of passages to study, I mostly choose ones which are controversial or difficult to understand.

8c When I give a testimony, I tend to emphasize the practical application of some verses to my life.

10a When conversing with other Christians, I tend to probe them to determine their true spiritual condition and needs.

11b When evaluating another Christian's spiritual condition, I tend to sense areas of right and wrong conduct in his life, and to point out some solutions.

15d If asked to lead in a church program somewhere, I would tend to choose a position which involved evaluating personnel for various leadership positions.

17c My reaction to the needs of others tends to be deliberate, because I want to make sure I've thought it through thoroughly.

18a In regard to decision making, I tend to make decisions easily and with confidence.

21c With regard to decisions made from my speaking, I prefer to have an opportunity to explore the decision in depth through discussion.

23d When called upon to serve, I am most naturally motivated to help in situations in which there are specific spiritual needs (for commitment, faith, dealing with sin, etc.).

25b Generally speaking, I have a tendency to be wise in discerning the character quality of another person.

25c Generally speaking, I have a tendency to accurately detect weaknesses and pitfalls when evaluating opportunities and situations.

25h Generally speaking, I have a tendency to see through others' actions to their real motives and inner attitudes.

VIII. *Gift of Helps*

2c I prefer speaking to individuals.

3a When faced with counseling another person about his problems, I tend to identify deeply with his situation.

5a When listening to others speak, I tend to be strongly impressed with exhortations to serve other Christians.

6c When I approach my personal devotions, I most prefer to relate to the verses emotionally, so as to get a personal blessing.

7b If I have my choice of passages to study, I mostly choose ones which are very practical.

8c When I give a testimony, I tend to emphasize the practical application of some verse(s) to my life.

12b When presented with a physical or spiritual need, I tend to respond best if someone calls and asks me to help fill it.

12c When presented with a physical or spiritual need, I tend to not respond if the need requires considerable personal preparation.

12d When presented with a physical or spiritual need, I tend to not respond if the need involves a lot of organizational detail and red tape.

13b In an organization, I prefer to be a follower under another's leadership.

14c When given a task which needs to be done now, I prefer to be told by a competent leader exactly what to do.

14e When given a task to do, I tend to favor doing it myself rather than delegating it.

16b If a group is meeting and no assigned leader is there, I would tend to let the meeting proceed with no direct leadership.

18c In regard to decision making when the facts are clear, I tend to rely on others whom I believe are more capable of sorting out the issues in the decision.

23a When called upon to serve, I am most naturally
motivated to help in situations in which there
are specific material needs (food, buildings,
equipment, money).

IX. *Gift of Serving*
2c I prefer speaking to individuals.
3a When faced with counseling another person
about his problems, I tend to identify deeply
with his situation.
5a When listening to others speak, I tend to dislike
in-depth doctrinal studies without applications.
5c When listening to others speak, I tend to be
strongly impressed with exhortations to serve
other Christians.
6c When I approach my personal devotions, I most
prefer to relate to the verses emotionally, so as
to get a personal blessing.
7b If I have my choice of passages to study, I
mostly choose ones which are very practical.
8c When I give a testimony, I tend to emphasize
the practical application of some verse(s) to my
life.
12a When presented with a physical or spiritual
need, I tend to respond on my own initiative to
try to meet it if I can.
12d When presented with a physical or spiritual
need, I tend to not respond if the need involves a
lot of organizational detail.
13a In an organization, I prefer to lead a group.
14b When given a task which needs to be done now,
I tend to leave it for another task if the second
one seems more important at the time.
14d When given a task which needs to be done now,
I tend to be concerned with doing a high quality
and thorough job.
14e When given a task to do, I tend to favor doing it
myself rather than delegating it.
16a If a group is meeting and no assigned leader is
there, I would tend to assume the leadership.
17b My reaction to the needs of others tends to be
quick because I usually sense what needs to be
done.

23a When called upon to serve, I am most naturally motivated to help in situations in which there are specific material needs (food, buildings, equipment, money).

25d Generally speaking, I have a tendency to have great energy and stamina for working on and meeting the practical needs of others.

X. Gift of Administration

1b I prefer situations in my church in which I am in a discussion group.

2b I prefer speaking to small groups.

9b With regard to planning for the future of my church, I tend to be concerned about and willing to do detailed, deliberate work on the plans.

11c When evaluating another Christian's spiritual condition, I tend to be critical of areas of his life which are not disciplined and well ordered.

13a In an organization, I prefer to lead a group.

14a When given a task which needs to be done now, I tend to complete it before taking on another task.

14d When given a task which needs to be done now, I tend to be concerned with doing a high quality and thorough job.

15c If asked to lead in a church program somewhere, I would tend to choose a position which involved harmonizing various viewpoints for a decision.

15b If asked to lead in a church program somewhere, I would tend to choose a position which involved detailed planning and decision making for the present.

15e If asked to lead in a church program somewhere, I would tend to choose a position which involved drawing up procedures and guidelines for effective inner working of the church.

16c If a group is meeting and no assigned leader is there, I would tend to appoint or ask someone in the group to lead.

17c My reaction to the needs of others tends to be deliberate because I want to make sure I've thought it through thoroughly.

18a In regard to decision making, I tend to make decisions easily and with confidence.

19d With regard to financial matters, I tend to feel deeply that such matters should be handled in an orderly and prudent manner.

22a If I were a leader faced with two Christians in the church who couldn't get along, I would tend to change one person's responsibilities and position at the point of conflict.

23a When called upon to serve, I am most naturally motivated to help in situations in which there are specific material needs (food, buildings, equipment, money).

XI. *Gift of Ruling*

1b I prefer situations in my church in which I am in a discussion group.

3b When faced with counseling another person about his problems, I tend to give him the best biblical solution I can think of, even if I'm not totally confident about my counsel.

5b When listening to others speak, I tend to dislike talks which heavily emphasize illustrations and applications without logical order and doctrine.

11c When evaluating another Christian's spiritual condition, I tend to be critical of areas of his/her life which are not disciplined and well ordered.

13a In an organization, I prefer to lead a group.

14a When given a task which needs to be done now, I tend to complete it before taking on another task.

14d When given a task which needs to be done now, I tend to be concerned with doing a high quality and thorough job.

15c If asked to lead in a church program somewhere, I would tend to choose a position which involved harmonizing various viewpoints for a decision.

15f If asked to lead in a church program somewhere, I would tend to choose a position which involved delegating responsibilities to others.

16a If a group is meeting and no assigned leader is there, I would tend to assume the leadership.

17c My reaction to the needs of others tends to be

deliberate because I want to make sure I've thought it through thoroughly.

18a In regard to decision making, I tend to make decisions easily and with confidence.

19d With regard to financial matters, I tend to feel deeply that such matters should be handled in an orderly and prudent manner.

22a If I were a leader faced with two Christians in the church who couldn't get along, I would tend to change one person's responsibilities and position at the point of conflict.

23a When called upon to serve, I am most naturally motivated to help in situations in which there are material needs (food, buildings, equipment, money, etc.).

25e Generally speaking, I have a tendency to be sensitive to overall organizational direction more than minority, individual opinions.

XII. Gift of Mercy

1c I prefer situations in my church in which I am only a listener.

2c I prefer speaking to individuals.

3a When faced with counseling another person about his problems, I tend to identify deeply with his situation.

3b When faced with counseling another person about his problems, I tend to give him the best biblical solution I can think of, even if I'm not totally confident about my counsel.

5c When listening to others speak, I tend to be strongly impressed by exhortations to serve other Christians.

6c When I approach my personal devotions, I mostly prefer to relate to the verses emotionally so as to get a personal blessing.

7b If I have my choice of passages to study, I mostly choose ones which are very practical.

7d If I have my choice of passages to study, I mostly choose ones which have great emotional appeal to my Christian life.

8a When I give a testimony, I tend to encourage or

console others rather than just share a verse or experience.

13b In an organization, I prefer to be a follower under another's leadership.

14e When given a task to do, I tend to favor doing it myself rather than delegating it.

17b My reaction to the needs of others tends to be quick, because I usually sense what needs to be done.

18b In regard to decision making, I tend to lack firmness because of people's feelings.

22c If I were a leader faced with two Christians in the church who couldn't get along, I would tend to leave the situation alone for fear of offending them and making it worse.

23c When called upon to serve, I am most naturally motivated to help in situations in which there are specific emotional needs (fear, anxiety, frustration, moods due to pain or trials, etc.).

25f Generally speaking, I have a tendency to help meet obvious needs without measuring the worthiness of the recipient or evaluating his real needs.

XIII. *Gift of Giving*

3a When faced with counseling another person about his problems, I tend to identify deeply with his situation.

5a When listening to others speak, I tend to dislike in-depth doctrinal studies without applications.

5c When listening to others speak, I tend to be strongly impressed with exhortations to serve other Christians.

6c When I approach my personal devotions, I most prefer to relate to the verses emotionally, so as to get a personal blessing.

7b If I have my choice of passages to study, I mostly choose ones which are very practical.

12a When presented with a physical or spiritual need, I tend to respond on my own initiative to try to meet it if I can.

12e When presented with a physical or spiritual problem, I tend to respond with money and possessions.

14e When given a task to do, I tend to favor doing it myself rather than delegating it.

17b My reaction to the needs of others tends to be quick because I usually sense what needs to be done.

19a With regard to financial matters, I tend to be able to make wise investments and gain wealth.

19b With regard to financial matters, I tend to be moved to give all I can to people and organizations I consider worthy.

19c With regard to financial matters, I tend to want assurances that the money I give will be used wisely.

19d With regard to financial matters, I tend to feel deeply that such matters should be handled in an orderly and prudent manner.

19f With regard to financial matters, I tend to work hard so I can meet legitimate needs.

23a When called upon to serve, I am most naturally motivated to help in situations in which there are specific material needs (food, buildings, equipment, etc.).

25g Generally speaking, I have a tendency to desire positive results and high quality in the things to which I give my efforts and money.

APPENDIX V
Guide to Interpreting
the Results of Evaluation Three

After you finish Evaluation Three, you may find that you still have not been able to gain clear direction regarding your gift. The percentage of circled responses may be very similar for three or four gifts. You must now analyze the responses so as to determine your predominant preferences and tendencies.

In the multiple choice setting, you may have selected preferences that were true, given the options. However, if your selected preferences had been compared with one another, probably one of them would have been stronger than the others.

The following analysis describes each gift in terms of the preferences and tendencies of one who possesses that gift. To use this analysis form, proceed in the following manner:

1. Note the name of the gifts for which you had similar preference percentages.
   a._____
   b._____
   c._____
   d._____
   e._____
2. Take the score sheet and locate the column with the name of the gift noted in 1a above. Proceed down the column in search of the circled X's. Whenever you find a circled X, move across the score sheet from the X to the far left-hand column where the numbered responses are given (2c, 3b, etc.).
3. After locating the numbered response corresponding to the circled X, proceed to the analysis of that gift below. Find the numbered response under the gift analysis which corresponds to the numbered response for the circled X in the score sheet. Circle that numbered response in the analysis.
4. Go back to the score sheet, find the second circled X and the corresponding numbered response, and circle that response under the same gift analysis below.
5. Repeat this procedure until all of the circled X's on

the score sheet are also circled under the gift analysis below.

6. Repeat the procedure in 2 above for each of the gifts noted in 1.

7. Then analyze the results by the following inquiry:

   a. Compare the circled responses of all the gifts analyzed in 2 above, noting when a particular preference or tendency has been circled under more than one gift. For example, if preaching and teaching were two of the gifts being analyzed, under the analysis both would have circled preference 1a: "I prefer situations in which I am a speaker." Since a number of gifts have the same preferences and tendencies, these should be noted.

   Gifts with the same   *Preferences used*
     preferences   *twice or more*

   *1)*_____   _____
   *2)*_____   _____
   *3)*_____   _____
   *4)*_____   _____
   *5)*_____   _____
   *6)*_____   _____
   *7)*_____   _____

   b. Think over the remaining preferences which have not been circled twice, and try to discern if there seem to be three or four responses which are not exactly the same preference but could be considered similar. Summarize the similar preferences and tendencies below.

   Gifts with similar
     preferences   *Summary*

   *1)*_____   _____
   *2)*_____   _____
   *3)*_____   _____

   c. Taking the results in a and b above, decide which of the gifts in 1 above is most like these same and similar preferences. The decision may be difficult, but always remember that the evaluation is to be used only as a guide for purposes of channeling you into service. The ultimate determination of your gift will take place through service.

   d. The same and similar preferences and tendencies along with overall analysis seem to indicate that my gift might be _____

GIFT ANALYSIS
IN TERMS OF PREFERENCES AND TENDENCIES

I. Gift of Prophecy (preaching)

1a He/she prefers situations in the church in which he/she is a speaker.

2a If asked to speak, he/she prefers to speak to large groups.

3b When faced with counseling another person about problems, he/she tends to give the person the best biblical solution he/she can think of, even if not totally confident about the counsel.

4a When he/she begins to prepare for talks to other Christians, he/she is normally motivated to emphasize the truths of basic Bible themes so as to lead the listeners to a clear-cut decision in the meeting.

5b When giving a testimony, he/she tends to indicate some area of doctrine that has come alive through an experience or a shared verse.

5c When he/she gives a testimony, he tends to emphasize the practical application of some verses to his/her life.

8a If a person were to ask him/her to evaluate another's spiritual condition, he/she would tend to point out errors in that person's mental understanding of the Christian life.

10a In an organization, he/she prefers to lead a group.

17d When called upon to serve, he/she is most naturally motivated to help in situations in which there are specific spiritual needs (for commitment, faith, dealing with sin, etc.).

18a When speaking before people, he/she has a tendency to try to persuade people to make spiritual decisions and commitments right then.

II. Gift of Teaching

1a He/she prefers situations in the church in which he/she is a speaker.

1b He/she prefers situations in the church in which he/she is in a discussion group.

2a If asked to speak, he/she prefers to speak to large groups.

2b If asked to speak, he/she prefers to speak to small groups.

3b When faced with counseling another person about problems, he/she tends to give the person the best biblical solution he/she can think of, even if not totally confident about the counsel.

4b When preparing for talks to other Christians, he/she is normally motivated to carefully organize a biblical passage in a systematic way so that the listeners clearly understand it.

5b When giving a testimony, he/she tends to indicate some area of doctrine that has come alive through an experience or a shared verse.

8a If a person were to ask him or her to evaluate another's spiritual condition, he/she would tend to point out errors in that person's mental understanding of the Christian life.

17b When called upon to serve, he/she is most naturally motivated to help in situations in which there are specific mental needs (lack of understanding of Scripture, need to find God's will in a certain area, etc.).

18b When speaking before people, he/she has a tendency to prepare well and speak carefully.

III. *Gift of Knowledge*

1b He/she prefers situations in the church in which he/she is in a discussion group.

2b If asked to speak, he/she prefers to speak to small groups.

3c When faced with counseling another person about problems, he/she tends to prefer sharing biblical insights, and avoiding discussions about feelings.

4c When preparing for talks to other Christians, he/she is normally motivated to instruct on doctrinal topics, to enable the listeners to have a better understanding of these subjects.

5b When giving a testimony, he/she tends to

indicate some area of doctrine that has come
alive through an experience or a shared verse.

8a If a person were to ask him/her to evaluate
another's spiritual condition, he/she would tend
to point out errors in that person's mental
understanding of the Christian life.

14a His/her reaction to the needs of others tends to
be slow, because of not knowing what to do.

17b When called upon to serve, he/she is most
naturally motivated to help in situations in
which there are specific mental needs (lack of
understanding of Scripture, need to find God's
will in a certain area, etc.).

18c When speaking before people, he/she has the
tendency to encourage thought-life decisions
more than conduct changes.

18d When speaking before people, he/she has a
tendency to have little interest in emotional
commitments unless they are based on clear
biblical teaching.

IV. *Gift of Wisdom*

1b He/she prefers situations in the church in which
he/she is in a discussion group.

2b If asked to speak, he/she prefers to speak to
small groups.

2c If asked to speak, he/she prefers to speak to
individuals.

3d When faced with counseling another person
about problems, he/she tends to urge the person
to follow his/her counsel, because he/she honestly
believes God helps him/her see the solutions to
others' problems.

4d When preparing for talks to other Christians,
he/she is normally motivated to stress
application of passages that emphasize practical
truths so that the listeners can refine their
conduct.

5a When giving a testimony, he/she tends to
encourage or console others rather than just
share a verse or experience.

5c When giving a testimony, he/she tends to
emphasize the practical application of some
verses to his/her life.

13c If a group is meeting and no assigned leader is there, he/she would tend to call someone to find out who the real leader is.

14c His/her reaction to the needs of others tends to be deliberate, because of wanting to make sure he/she has thought it through thoroughly.

17b When called upon to serve, he/she is most naturally motivated to help in situations in which there are specific mental needs (lack of understanding of Scripture, need to find God's will in a certain area, etc.).

V. *Gift of Exhortation*

1b He/she prefers situations in the church in which he/she is in a discussion group.

2a If asked to speak, he/she prefers to speak to large groups.

3a When faced with counseling another person about problems, he/she tends to identify deeply with the person's situation.

3d When faced with counseling another person about problems, he/she tends to urge the person to follow the counsel, because he/she honestly believes God helps him/her see the solutions to others' problems.

4e When he/she begins to prepare for talks to other Christians, he/she is normally motivated to take one verse and outline practical and specific steps of action for the listener to follow.

5a When giving a testimony, he/she tends to encourage or console others, rather than just share a verse or experience.

7b When conversing with other Christians, he/she tends to exhort them to embrace certain goals and actions.

8b If a person asks him/her to evaluate another's spiritual condition, he/she would tend to sense areas of right and wrong conduct in that person's life, and to point out some solutions.

14b His/her reaction to the needs of others tends to be quick, because he/she usually senses what needs to be done.

17c When called upon to serve, he/she is most

naturally motivated to help in situations in which there are specific emotional needs (fear, anxiety, frustration, moods due to pain and trials, etc.).

VI. Gift of Faith

1b He/she prefers situations in the church in which he/she is in a discussion group.

2b If asked to speak, he/she prefers to speak to small groups.

3b When faced with counseling another person about problems, he/she tends to give the person the best biblical solution he/she can think of, even if not totally confident about the counsel.

6a With regard to planning for the future of his/her church, he/she tends to have positive confidence about what the church should do.

6b With regard to planning for the future of his/her church, he/she tends to be more concerned with envisioning end results than with the details involved in getting there.

6c With regard to planning for the future of his/her church, he/she tends to have a great desire to see quick growth in the ministries of the church.

7b When conversing with other Christians, he/she tends to exhort them to embrace certain goals and actions.

14b His/her reaction to the needs of others tends to be quick, because he/she senses what needs to be done most of the time.

16d With regard to financial matters, he/she tends to be moved to give all he can to people and organizations he/she considers worthy.

17d When called upon to serve, he/she is most naturally motivated to help in situations in which there are specific spiritual needs (for commitment, faith, dealing with sin, etc.).

VII. Gift of Discernment of Spirits

1b He/she prefers situations in the church in which he/she is in a discussion group.

2b If asked to speak, he/she prefers to speak to small groups.

3d When faced with counseling another person

about problems, he/she tends to urge the person to follow his counsel, because he/she honestly believes God helps him/her see the solutions to others' problems.

5c When giving a testimony, he/she tends to emphasize the practical application of some verses to his/her life.

7a When conversing with other Christians, he/she tends to probe them to determine their true spiritual condition and needs.

8b If a person asks him/her to evaluate another's spiritual condition, he/she would tend to sense areas of right and wrong conduct in that person's life, and to point out some solutions.

12c If asked to lead somewhere in the church program, he/she would tend to choose a position which involved evaluating personnel for various leadership positions.

14c His/her reaction to the needs of others tends to be deliberate, because of wanting to make sure he/she has thought it through thoroughly.

17d When called upon to serve, he/she is most naturally motivated to help in situations in which there are specific spiritual needs (for commitment, faith, dealing with sin, etc.).

VIII. *Gift of Helps*

2c If asked to speak, he/she prefers to speak to individuals.

3a When faced with counseling another person about problems, he/she tends to identify deeply with the person's situation.

5c When giving a testimony, he/she tends to emphasize the practical application of some verses to his/her life.

9b When presented with a physical or spiritual need, he/she tends to respond best if someone calls and asks him/her to help.

9c When presented with a physical or spiritual need, he/she tends to not respond if the need requires some time for personal preparation.

10b In an organization, he/she prefers to be a follower under another's leadership.

11c When given a task which needs to be done now,
he/she tends to favor doing it himself/herself
rather than delegating it.

13b If a group is meeting and no assigned leader is
there, he/she would tend to let the meeting
proceed with no direct leadership.

15b In regard to decision making when the facts are
clear, he/she tends to rely on others whom
he/she believes are more capable of sorting out
the issues in the decision.

17a When called upon to serve, he/she is most
naturally motivated to help in situations in
which there are specific material needs (food,
buildings, equipment, money).

IX. *Gift of Serving*

3a When faced with counseling another person
about problems, he/she tends to identify deeply
with the person's situation.

5c When giving a testimony, he/she tends to
emphasize the practical application of some
verses to his/her life.

9a When presented with a physical or spiritual
need, he/she tends to respond on his own
initiative to try to meet it if possible.

10a In an organization, he/she prefers to lead a
group.

11a When given a task which needs to be done now,
he/she tends to leave it for another task if the
second one seems more important at the time.

11b When given a task which needs to be done now,
he/she tends to be concerned with doing a high
quality and thorough job.

11c When given a task which needs to be done now,
he/she tends to favor doing it himself/herself
rather than delegating it.

13a If a group is meeting and no assigned leader is
there, he/she would tend to assume the
leadership.

14b His/her reaction to the needs of others tends to
be quick, because he/she usually senses what
needs to be done.

17a When called upon to serve, he/she is most

naturally motivated to help in situations in which there are specific material needs (food, buildings, equipment, money).

X. *Gift of Administration*

1b He/she prefers situations in the church in which he/she is in a discussion group.

2b If asked to speak, he/she prefers to speak to small groups.

8c If a person asks him/her to evaluate another's spiritual condition, he/she would tend to be critical of areas of that person's life which are not disciplined and well ordered.

10a In an organization, he/she prefers to lead a group.

11b When given a task which needs to be done now, he/she tends to be concerned with doing a high quality and thorough job.

12a If asked to lead in the church program somewhere, he/she would tend to choose a position which involves detailed planning and decision making for the present.

12b If asked to lead in the church program somewhere, he/she would tend to choose a position which involves harmonizing various viewpoints for a decision.

14c His/her reaction to the needs of others tends to be deliberate, because of wanting to make sure he/she has thought it through thoroughly.

16c With regard to financial matters, he/she tends to feel deeply that such matters should be handled in an orderly and prudent manner.

17a When called upon to serve, he/she is most naturally motivated to help in situations in which there are specific material needs (food, buildings, equipment, money).

XI. *Gift of Ruling*

1a He/she prefers situations in the church in which he/she is a speaker.

3b When faced with counseling another person about problems, he/she tends to give the person the best biblical solution he/she can think of, even if not totally confident about the counsel.

8c If a person asks him/her to evaluate another's spiritual condition, he/she would tend to be critical of areas of that person's life which are not disciplined and well ordered.

10a In an organization, he/she prefers to lead a group.

11b When given a task which needs to be done now, he/she tends to be concerned with doing a high quality and thorough job.

12b If asked to lead somewhere in the church program, he/she would tend to choose a position which involves harmonizing various viewpoints for a decision.

13a If a group is meeting and no assigned leader is there, he/she would tend to assume the leadership.

14c His/her reaction to the needs of others tends to be deliberate, because of wanting to make sure he/she has thought it through thoroughly.

16c With regard to financial matters, he/she tends to feel deeply that such matters should be handled in an orderly and prudent manner.

17a When called upon to serve, he/she is most naturally motivated to help in situations in which there are specific material needs (foods, buildings, equipment, money).

XII. *Gift of Mercy*

1c He/she prefers situations in the church in which he/she is just a listener.

2c If asked to speak, he/she prefers to speak to individuals.

3a When faced with counseling another person about problems, he/she tends to identify deeply with the person's situation.

3b When faced with counseling another person about problems, he/she tends to give the person the best biblical solution he/she can think of, even if not totally confident about the counsel.

5a When giving a testimony, he/she tends to encourage or console others, rather than just share a verse or experience.

10b In an organization, he/she prefers to be a follower under another's leadership.

11c When given a task which needs to be done now, he/she tends to favor doing it himself/herself rather than delegating it.

14b His/her reaction to the needs of others tends to be quick, because he/she usually senses what needs to be done.

15a In regard to decision making when the facts are clear, he/she tends to lack firmness because of people's feelings.

17c When called upon to serve, he/she is most naturally motivated to help in situations in which there are specific emotional needs (fear, anxiety, frustration, moods due to pain and trials, etc.).

XIII. *Gift of Giving*

3a When faced with counseling another person about problems, he/she tends to identify deeply with the person's situation.

9a When presented with a physical or spiritual need, he/she tends to respond on his/her own initiative to try to meet it if possible.

9d When presented with a physical or spiritual need, he/she tends to respond with money and possessions.

11c When given a task which needs to be done now, he/she tends to favor doing it himself/herself rather than delegating it.

14b His/her reaction to the needs of others tends to be quick, because he/she usually senses what needs to be done.

16a With regard to financial matters, he/she tends to be able to make wise investments and gain wealth.

16b With regard to financial matters, he/she tends to be moved to give generously to people and organizations he/she considers worthy.

16c With regard to financial matters, he/she tends to feel deeply that such matters should be handled in an orderly and prudent manner.

16e With regard to financial matters, he/she tends to work hard to meet legitimate needs.

17a When called upon to serve, he/she is most

naturally motivated to help in situations in which there are specific material needs (food, buildings, equipment, money).

4